WORLD BANK WORKING PAPER NO. 73

Gender, Time Use, and Poverty in Sub-Saharan Africa

Edited by C. Mark Blackden and Quentin Wodon

THE WORLD BANK
Washington, D.C.

World Bank Working Papers are published to communicate the results of the Bank's work to the development community with the least possible delay. The manuscript of this paper therefore has not been prepared in accordance with the procedures appropriate to formally-edited texts. Some sources cited in this paper may be informal documents that are not readily available.

ISBN-10: 0-8213-6561-4   ISBN-13: 978-0-8213-6561-8
eISBN: 0-8213-6562-2
ISSN: 1726-5878   DOI: 10.1596/978-0-8213-6561-8

Cover Photo by C. Mark Blackden. Batik from Burkina Faso, c. 1996. Artist unknown, presented as a gift to Callisto Madavo.

C. Mark Blackden and Quentin Wodon are Lead Specialists in the Office of the Sector Director, Poverty Reduction and Economic Management, Africa Region of the World Bank.

Library of Congress Cataloging-in-Publication Data has been requested.

Contents

LIST OF FIGURES

LIST OF BOXES

Foreword

Gender, Time Use, and Poverty in Sub-Saharan Africa sheds light on a critical dimension of poverty in Sub-Saharan Africa: time poverty. Although the concept of time poverty has been used in the development literature, it is not always clear what is meant by time poverty, how it can be measured, what impact it has on other areas, and what actions are most effective in addressing it. This volume tackles these questions by exploring the concept of time poverty, reviewing existing studies on time use in Africa, developing tools and approaches for analyzing time use and time poverty, and assessing the impact of time use and time poverty on other development indicators. The insights provided in the various papers included in this volume show that a better understanding of time poverty is required to inform poverty diagnostics, national poverty reduction strategies, and the design and implementation of development interventions.

As argued by the editors of the volume in their introduction, the lack of data on time use and the omission of the household economy from conventional development planning mean that the picture of the development process is incomplete and our understanding of the labor supply of households is insufficient—much of what we are (or should be) concerned with occurs in an invisible realm. There is therefore a tendency to make misleading assumptions about labor availability and labor mobility. Overlooking the differences in men's and women's contributions to "household time overhead" can lead to inappropriate policies which have the unintended effect of raising women's labor burdens while sometimes lowering those of men. Furthermore, as a community of policymakers and development practitioners, we often do not invest in (or prioritize) what is not visible: so if the household economy is not visible to policymakers and planners, they are unlikely to prioritize investment in it. This means that we do not recognize the tradeoffs or positive links among different tasks and activities, and, by extension, do not focus on reducing or minimizing the tradeoffs and on building on the positive linkages.

The papers in this volume outline a challenging agenda for Africa. For example, seasonality in rural work and the combination of underemployment and labor shortages within a given population at different times of the year call for appropriately designed policy responses and programs. The issue of care for sufferers of HIV/AIDS needs to be analyzed further and integrated into the response to the pandemic. The wider question of care, how care work is captured, how it interacts with other domestic and other work, also needs more attention in both time use surveys and in policy responses. Finally, infrastructure investments, already recognized as a priority in the World Bank's Africa Action Plan, need to be directed in part toward meeting the requirements of household production and the household economy, and helping women to reduce their time burdens. Acting on this agenda will help governments in prioritizing public actions aimed at accelerating progress toward the targets laid out in the Millennium Development Goals.

Sudhir Shetty
Sector Director, Poverty Reduction and Economic Management
Africa Region, World Bank

Abstract

The papers in this volume examine the links between gender, time use, and poverty in Sub-Saharan Africa. They contribute to a broader definition of poverty to include "time poverty," and to a broader definition of work to include household work. The papers present a conceptual framework linking both market and household work, review some of the available literature and surveys on time use in Africa, and use tools and approaches drawn from analysis of consumption-based poverty to develop the concept of a time poverty line and to examine linkages between time poverty, consumption poverty, and other dimensions of development in Africa such as education and child labor.

Acknowledgments

This volume was prepared by C. Mark Blackden and Quentin Wodon, in the Office of the Sector Director, Poverty Reduction and Economic Management, Africa Region. Two of the chapters in the volume draw on work commissioned by the World Bank from the International Center for Research on Women (ICRW), which was carried out by Jacques Charmes (Consultant, Institut de Recherche le Développement, Paris), and by Aslihan Kes and Hema Swaminathan, with support from Caren Grown and Elizabeth Nicoletti. The rest of the papers in the volume draw on work undertaken by the Poverty Team in the Africa Region as part of contributions to poverty assessments for Guinea, Malawi, and Rwanda. These papers were prepared by Elena Bardasi, Kathleen Beegle, Corinne Siaens, Kalanidhi Subbarao, and Quentin Wodon.

We gratefully acknowledge the comments and guidance provided by the peer reviewers for the papers, namely Andrew Morrison (PRMGE) for the papers in Part I of the volume and Kathleen Beegle (DECRG) for the papers in Parts II and III except the Malawi paper that was reviewed by Antonio Nucifora (AFTP1) and the Rwanda paper that was reviewed by Kene Ezemenari (AFTP3) and Bruno Boccara (AFTP3). A workshop to discuss the papers in this volume was held at the World Bank in November 2005, and the papers benefited greatly from the many thoughtful comments and ideas from the participants at this workshop. We also thank Alfia Johnson and Hilda Emeruwa for their valuable support in organizing the workshop.

Financial support was provided by two trust funds. The first trust fund is the Norwegian/Netherlands fund for gender mainstreaming (GENFUND), which provided an important impetus to launch this work to address time use issues in poverty analysis, and which has supported the publication and dissemination of this volume. The second trust fund is the Belgian Poverty Reduction Partnership (BPRP), which provided support for papers in Parts II and III of the volume.

This work was prepared under the overall leadership of Paula Donovan, former Sector Director, PREM, Africa, who unstintingly encouraged greater synergy between work on poverty and work on gender in the Africa Region.

CHAPTER 1

Gender, Time Use, and Poverty: Introduction

C. Mark Blackden and Quentin Wodon

This volume aims to shed light on the question of "time poverty" in Sub-Saharan Africa and its relationship with consumption-based measures of poverty, as well as other development outcomes. Time poverty, especially as seen in the "double workday" of women, has long been a staple of discussion of women's situation in Africa. Yet it is not always clear what is meant by time poverty, how time poverty is measured, or what actions are required to tackle time poverty once identified. The papers presented in this volume seek to address these questions by reviewing the existing literature and analyzing new data available in time use modules of household income and consumption surveys in several African countries. The objective is to provide guidance and examples of how to define and measure time poverty, and also to address ways through which a better understanding of time poverty can inform poverty diagnostics, national poverty reduction strategies, and the design and implementation of development interventions.

Time Use and Africa's Development

Perhaps nowhere is the asymmetry in the respective rights and obligations of men and women more apparent than in the patterns of time use differentiated by gender, and the inefficiency and inequity they represent. Both men and women play multiple roles (productive, reproductive, and community management) in society (Moser 1989; Blackden and Bhanu 1999). Yet while men are generally able to focus on a single productive role, and play their multiple roles sequentially, women, in contrast to men, play these roles simultaneously and must balance simultaneous competing claims on limited time for each of them. Women's labor time and flexibility are therefore much more constrained than is the case for men. Comparative time use data reflect these constraints, though it is particularly difficult to capture "simultaneous" tasks and to measure the "intensity" of work, whether for men or for women. The gender division of labor defines women's and men's economic opportunities, and determines their capacity to allocate labor time for economically productive activities and to respond to economic incentives. Although some of these differences in time allocation can be explained through economic factors, in many societies these are secondary to non-economic factors in determining time use patterns (Ilahi 2000).

Gender-differentiated time use patterns are affected by many factors, including household composition and life cycle issues (age and gender composition of household members), seasonal and farm system considerations, regional and geographic factors, including ease of access to water and fuel, availability of infrastructure, and distance to key economic and social services such as schools, health centers, financial institutions, and markets. But social and cultural norms also play an important role both in defining, and sustaining rigidity in, the gender division of labor. This is most evident in the division of responsibilities between productive (market) and reproductive (household) work. In addition to their prominence in agriculture and in much of the informal sector, women bear the brunt of domestic tasks: processing food crops, providing water and firewood, and caring for the elderly and the sick, this latter activity assuming much greater significance in the face of the HIV/AIDS pandemic. The time and effort required for these tasks, in the almost total absence of even rudimentary domestic technology, is staggering.[1]

It is important to examine time use in Sub-Saharan Africa and to address its policy and operational implications for at least three reasons. First, time use data in Sub-Saharan African countries show what people actually do in their daily lives, and therefore provide important information on work and on labor allocation within households. Second, in doing this, they make apparent not only that there is a division of labor, in that different people do different things, but also that differences in how men and women use their time are of considerable importance in understanding poverty in Africa—the gender division of labor is especially significant. Third, time allocation data reveal not only the substantial market economy contributions of men and women to Africa's development, but also, and just as importantly, the existence of a whole realm of human activity—what is termed here the "household economy"—that is largely invisible and uncounted in economic data and in the system of national accounts (SNA).[2]

Examination of time use data therefore performs the critically important function of giving policymakers and development practitioners a much more complete and comprehensive picture of employment and labor effort than would otherwise be afforded by labor force data alone. This is done by making visible and providing quantified estimates of non-market contributions to total household production and welfare, alongside market-based

---

1. Some studies have found high correlation between opportunity costs to the household of children's time and enrollment figures. In Tanzania, on average, the opportunity cost for families to send girls to schools is significantly higher than that of boys. If boys from 13 to 15 years old are in school, households lose about 25 hours of work per week. For girls of the same age, they lose about 37 hours of work (World Bank 1999). Boys may drop out of school to herd, farm, fish, hunt or to engage in petty trade. For girls, the main reasons for dropping out are pregnancy, parental concerns about toilet facilities, long distances, and lack of security.

2. Ironmonger estimates, for example, that labor market employment statistics cover less than 50 percent of all work performed, and that the regularly published labor statistics cover perhaps 75 percent of men's work and 33 percent of women's work. See Ironmonger (1999).

work. Because these contributions are essential for family survival, it is important for policymakers and development practitioners to focus on them explicitly. Non-market labor is of particular importance from a gender standpoint, as the household economy is where women predominantly work.

One of the most important insights from gender analysis of time use in Sub-Saharan Africa is that there are synergies, and short-term tradeoffs, between and within market-oriented and household-oriented activities—economic production, childbearing and rearing, and household/community management responsibilities. These assume particular importance because of the competing claims on women's labor time in most environments. There are interconnections between rural development and transport (Barwell 1996), between education, health, and fertility, between girls' education and domestic tasks, and within the population/agriculture/environment "nexus" (Cleaver and Schreiber 1994). Other critical interconnections illuminated by time use studies exist between the time spent (mainly by women and very young children) preparing and cooking meals in degraded and polluted environments and health, as reflected in high levels of acute respiratory infections related to exposure to air pollutants (for an articulation of this issue in Uganda, see Green 2005). Several studies document that workload constraints limit the likelihood that children will be taken to health posts for vaccinations, or that sick children or family members will access health care in a timely manner. As argued by the World Bank (2006), there is a critically small "window of opportunity" for addressing undernutrition in children, which in turn hinges on timely access to food, including time for breastfeeding and timely preparation of meals in the first two years of life—a period in which, according to time use survey data, women with young children are likely to be especially heavily burdened with work. Building on these cross-sectoral interconnections can have positive multiplier effects for growth and poverty reduction.

A related insight is that some time uses are indispensable, as argued by Harvey and Taylor (2000) when they refer to "household time overhead." This concept refers to the minimum number of hours that a household must spend on the basic chores vital to the survival of the family, that is, the time spent preparing meals, washing clothes, cleaning, fetching water, and gathering fuel for cooking and heating. They argue that, in general, a household with low household time overhead will be better off than a household with high time overhead, though they recognize that the impact of the time overhead will in turn depend on the number of adults and children available to assist in performing these tasks.

Tradeoffs in time allocation, and sometimes harsh choices, are at the core of the interrelationship between the "visible" market and "invisible" household economies, given the simultaneous competing claims on women's—but not men's—labor time. There are tradeoffs between different productive activities, between market and household tasks, and between meeting short-term economic and household needs and long-term investment in future capacity and human capital. The work burden on women, and the disproportionate cost borne by women of reproductive work in the household economy not only limits the time women can spend in economic activities but restricts them (spatially and culturally) to activities compatible with their domestic obligations (Blackden and Morris-Hughes 1993). A review of the relationship between female headship and poverty found that the reasons for greater poverty among female-maintained families lie not in structural factors in household composition, such as higher dependency ratios, or in gender-related differences in economic opportunity, but in the combination of the two. Where women heads of households have no other adult women to fulfill home production or domestic roles, they face greater time and mobility constraints than do male heads or other women, that in turn leads to lower paying jobs more compatible with childcare (Buvinic and Rao Gupta 1997). The review cites evidence from Malawi indicating that female farmers were inclined to limit their labor time in farm activities due to a heavy commitment to domestic chores, while responsibility for children and housekeeping made it difficult for female heads to opt for regular or off-farm labor activities to increase their earnings. Because they must carry out their multiple roles simultaneously, and because the "household time overhead" is not dispensable, women can only engage in directly productive economic activity (whether measured or not) after or in conjunction with the discharge of their domestic responsibilities. Balancing competing time uses, in a framework of almost total inelasticity of the gender division of labor, presents a particular challenge to reducing poverty. In many circumstances, necessary and essential actions, including both directly productive tasks and meeting the "household time overhead," must *compete* for scarce labor time.

Here too, though, the situation is not necessarily straightforward. The idea that poverty is a function of time as well as money is not new, as this was articulated by Vickery in 1977 (see Harvey and Taylor 2000). Time poverty and income poverty may reinforce each other with negative consequences for individual and household well-being. For example, the sheer drudgery and low productivity of many non-market tasks, which are time- and labor-intensive, reduces the availability of time for household members engaged in such tasks to participate in more economically productive activities. Given that such tasks are primarily carried out by women, this means that women in particular are less likely to be able to take full advantage of economic opportunities, to respond to changing market conditions and incentives, and to participate in income-generating activities.[3] Time poverty also impedes individuals' ability to expand their capabilities through education and skills development that could enhance economic returns in the market place. However, the question can also be asked in a different way, namely: to what extent could more time spent working (but without making a larger share of the population time poor) help reduce poverty? The logic is then inverted, by showing that even if many men and women work a lot, there may be a reserve of time that, if jobs were available, could be tapped to reduce consumption poverty. Said differently, there are circumstances in which underemployment is widespread, at least at certain periods of the year, and "time poverty" as such does not appear to be the main constraint that prevents the consumption poor to escape poverty.

The above discussion suggests that the time problem is a key component of the more traditional poverty problem, and one which deserves more attention in poverty diagnostics and Poverty Reduction Strategy Papers. A possible avenue for further research is to define more precisely the "household time overhead" and to link it with other dimensions of time use. This would allow for more exact specification of when the household time

---

3. The wider set of issues linking gender inequality and economic growth are beyond the scope of this paper. Discussion of these issues can be found in World Bank (2001), Blackden and Bhanu (1999), and Gelb (2001).

overhead becomes a constraint on labor use for other tasks, and constitutes a form of time poverty even in environments of under- or unemployment where total time use does not appear to be a constraint. More generally, omission of the household economy from conventional development planning means that:

- The picture is incomplete and our understanding of the total labor effort of households is insufficient—much of what we are (or should be) concerned with occurs in this invisible realm;
- There is a tendency to make misleading assumptions about labor availability and labor mobility treating, for example, women's capacity to undertake unpaid domestic labor as "infinitely elastic" (Elson 1993)—overlooking the differences in men's and women's contributions to household time overhead can lead to inappropriate policies which have the unintended effect of raising women's labor burdens while sometimes lowering those of men;
- We do not invest in (or prioritize) what is not there—if the household economy is not visible to policymakers and planners, they are unlikely to prioritize investment in it; and
- We do not see the tradeoffs among different tasks and activities, and, by extension, do not place reducing or minimizing these tradeoffs at the core of our response— nor do we see sufficiently the positive linkages, and prioritize the benefits from these linkages in our actions.

Brief Overview of the Contributions in This Volume

Many of the above considerations were reflected in the policy research report "Engendering Development" (World Bank 2001) that addressed the link between time poverty and income poverty as well as growth. Indeed, "time poverty" is not a new concept. Time constraints have been articulated as a central development problem for Africa for many years. Data from two village surveys in the Central African Republic in 1960 confirm the longevity of gender-differentiated time allocation burdens. In one village, men work 5.5 hours per day, women more than 8 (Berio, 1983). The conclusion of this study is particularly interesting: Rural modernization for improving productivity increases women's workload and reduces men's working hours. "In these conditions, any programme of rural modernization will soon reach its limits, unless planners can force men to work more on agriculture, and also to release women from part of their workload." Time—women's time in particular—can be the scarce production factor in a development process.

The papers presented in this volume are intended to make a contribution to a long-standing debate and field of analysis. The first part of the volume comprises two papers devoted to reviews of the literature and empirical evidence to date on time use and time poverty in Sub-Saharan Africa (SSA). Chapter 2 presents an overview of the "time poverty" problem in SSA. It presents a simplified conceptual framework for analysis of the overlapping domains of work, when market-based and non-market work are combined into a more comprehensive view of total household production. It discusses methodological issues associated with time use surveys, paying particular attention to questions of how work is defined in different frameworks (a topic that is addressed further in Chapter 3).

It also raises issues relating to how intensity of work, and simultaneity of tasks can be captured in time use surveys, and how this can be pursued in analysis. The paper then reviews some of the available literature in SSA on time use, paying particular attention to time problems associated with care for people suffering from HIV/AIDS, and the paper finds that this issue has not received sufficient attention in time use analysis, despite its clear significance in SSA. This is clearly an area requiring much more research and analysis in future, to inform strategies for coping, treatment, and mitigation of the effects of HIV/ AIDS. The paper focuses in particular on the importance of developing infrastructure in SSA in ways that are more closely aligned with alleviating the time burdens of household economy production and which are accessible to women, so that they specifically lessen their time burdens.

Chapter 3 picks up on the question of how work is defined, and traces the more recent changes in, and limitations of, the System of National Accounts (SNA), in terms of how these changes capture unpaid non-market work. While some unpaid work is included in the SNA (defined as "contributing" labor), there is still a considerable amount of unpaid, non-market work in the household economy that is not in the SNA, and that is, economically speaking, invisible. The chapter then documents the findings of national time use surveys in several SSA countries, which provide a descriptive foundation for looking more widely at total household production. What these surveys tell us, along with much of the other time use literature in SSA, is how extensive and significant such non-market, unpaid time use is, and that the household economy, if counted, would be one of the largest economic sectors in terms of the labor (time) allocated to it, and the output that it produces.

Part II of the volume comprises two chapters devoted to the measurement of time poverty, with data from Guinea and Malawi. In Chapter 4, it is argued that the availability of better data on time use in developing countries makes it important to provide tools for analyzing such data. While the idea of "time poverty" is not new, and while many studies have provided measures of time use and hinted at the concept of time poverty, we have not seen in the literature formal discussions and measurement of the concept of time poverty alongside the techniques used for measuring consumption poverty. Conceptually, time poverty can be understood as the fact that some individuals do not have enough time for rest and leisure after taking into account the time spent working, whether in the labor market, for domestic work, or for other activities such as fetching water and wood. Said differently, for those who are working long hours, the time constraint makes it necessary for individuals to make hard choices in terms of to what they allocate their time, with these hard choices having implications for the welfare of individuals and the household to which they belong. Unlike consumption or income, where economists assume that "more is better," time is a limited resource—more time spent working in paid or unpaid work-related activities means less leisure, and therefore higher "time poverty." The objective of Chapter 4 is to demonstrate with data from Guinea how one may apply the concepts used in the consumption poverty literature to time use, in order to obtain measures of time poverty for a population as a whole and for various groups of individuals.

Chapter 5 is devoted to the issue of seasonality in time use with an exploration of data from Malawi. The available empirical evidence for Malawi and for many other developing countries suggests the existence of labor shortages at the peak of the cropping season, with negative impacts on the ability of households to make the most of their endowments such as land. At the same time, for most of the year, there is substantial underemployment, especially in rural areas. It could therefore be argued that seasonality in the demand for labor is leading to both underemployment and labor shortages. To assess the validity of this argument, Chapter 5 provides basic descriptive data from a 2004 nationally-representative household survey to assess the typical workload of the population. The data do confirm the presence of strong seasonality effects in the supply of labor, as well as substantial differences in workload between men and women due to the burden of domestic work, including the time spent for collecting water and wood.

The last part of the volume also comprises two chapters devoted to the implications of time use and time poverty for development outcomes. Chapter 6 looks at the link between underemployment and consumption-based poverty. Despite already long working hours for many household members, and especially women, underemployment is nevertheless affecting a large share of the population in many developing countries. Using the same data on time use as in Chapter 4, as well as data on wages and consumption levels from the household survey for Guinea, the chapter provides a simple framework for assessing the potential impact on poverty and inequality of an increase in the working hours of the population up to what is referred to as a full employment workload. The framework provides for a decomposition of the contribution to higher household consumption of an increase in working hours for both men and women. The key message is that job creation and full employment would lead to a significant reduction in poverty, even at the relatively low current levels of wages and earnings enjoyed by the population. However, even at full employment levels, poverty would remain massive, and the higher workload that the full employment scenario would entail would be significant.

Finally, Chapter 7 looks at the links between welfare, time use, and other development outcomes in a case study of orphans in Rwanda. One of the aspects of the orphan crisis in Sub-Saharan Africa indeed relates to time use, both in terms of where orphans end up living and what they spend their time doing in their new household of adoption and in terms of the burdens of care. While some orphans are welcomed in centers and institutions, many live with relatives or other members of their communities, and some others are welcomed by families which are not directly related to them. Orphans are in many ways better off when welcomed by relatives or other families than when living by themselves or in institutions, but there are also concerns that the orphans (and especially girls) that are welcomed in some families may be required to provide more help for the domestic tasks to be performed, with the resulting time pressure in terms of workload preventing them from benefitting from the same opportunities in education and other aspects of their development as other children. The objective of the chapter is to conduct preliminary work to test this assumption using recent household survey data from Rwanda, paying attention not only to traditional variables of interest such as school enrollment, child labor and time use, but also with an eye to assessing other dimensions of welfare.

What Next? Some Areas for Further Research

A workshop was held at the World Bank in November 2005 to discuss all the papers presented in this volume except the Rwanda case study (which was added to broaden the scope of this volume), and to raise issues and concerns relating to the concept, measurement, and implications of "time poverty." Some of the key points raised at the workshop are summarized below. Participants noted that even the descriptive data on comparative time uses of men and women were striking in revealing gender-differentiated work burdens, especially in relation to how things have evolved in the context of HIV/AIDS, and notwithstanding the continued lack of adequate data in this area. Shaping the analytical agenda was of concern to many participants, including making better use of existing data, generating new data, and linking the discussion of time poverty to the wider questions of gender inequality in access to and control of resources, addressing the implications of time poverty for women's labor force participation, looking at child labor issues, and tackling the operational question of what investments are required to have the maximum positive impact on reducing time poverty and improving other development outcomes, especially those related to the Millennium Development Goals.

A related set of concerns articulated at the workshop was to pay explicit attention to the time demands of development programs, and to look in a more focused manner at what development outcomes are affected by time poverty. This was especially the case with respect to health and child welfare. Some participants suggested that beyond the definition of a time poverty line (a specific amount of time worked), it will be important to pay more attention to the productivity of time use and to the ways in which time is used. In addition, it was pointed out that in some situations, not having the time (opportunity) to engage in directly productive work can also be seen as an important issue (related to underemployment), just as working more hours and earning more can often be seen as a good thing. Data quality, measurement error, classification of tasks, and capturing both simultaneity and intensity of work, were also raised by participants as issues for further work. These issues all merit further attention in taking the analysis of time poverty forward.

Key challenges identified at the workshop include that of communicating effectively what the time poverty problem is, and how to address it. It is critical to focus attention on development outcomes (informing the "results agenda") that time poverty most affects. This in turn requires much more focus on technology, including labor-saving technology accessible to women to reduce the burden and drudgery of household tasks. In this context, the renewed focus on infrastructure, for example in the World Bank's Africa Action Plan, while welcome, needs to be directed toward meeting the specific needs of the household economy.

For example, the gender division of labor in transport tasks, as revealed in time allocation data, leaves women with by far the most substantial transport task in rural areas. These figures equate to a time input for an average adult female ranging from just under 1 hour to 2 hours 20 minutes every day. Water, firewood, and crops for grinding are transported predominantly by women on foot, the load normally being carried on the head. Village transport surveys in Ghana, Tanzania, and Zambia show that women spend nearly three times as much time in transport activities compared with men, and they transport about four times as much in volume (Malmberg-Calvo 1994). What would happen if all households in SSA were no more than 400 m (about a six minute walk) from a potable water source—a national target once set by the Government of Tanzania—or if woodlots or other sources of household energy were no farther than a 30-minute walk? Barwell (1996) summarizes the results of such analysis in five settings. In the Mbale district in Eastern Uganda, more than 900 hours/year could be saved if these proximity targets were met. This represents a considerable outlay of household time and energy, predominantly by women, amounting to the equivalent of a half year of 40-hour work weeks.

Public policies could have a significant impact on the heavy time burden of domestic work through investment in the household economy. Such investment would aim to reduce the "household time overhead" discussed earlier, and thereby directly relieve the time burdens on women and reduce the tradeoffs among competing uses of scarce labor. Infrastructure to provide clean and accessible water supply, and energy focused on domestic requirements (notably for cooking fuel) is especially critical, in view of its multiple benefits. Labor-saving domestic technology relating to food processing is likely to have a greater immediate impact in raising the productivity and reducing the time burdens of many women. Transport interventions need to reflect the different needs of men and women, so as to improve women's access to transport services (including intermediate means of transport), commensurate with their load-carrying responsibilities. These investments in the household economy have substantial payoffs in increased efficiency and growth in the market economy. Energy policy and investment priorities need to focus on alternative energy sources, and to address the domestic energy needs of households, especially as concerns fuel for cooking. This will have important multiplier effects on improving health, saving time, and enabling girls to go to (and stay) in school. Investing in labor-saving technologies accessible to women, and focused on reducing the considerable time and effort expended to transform and process agricultural and food products—a time expenditure often greater than the time required to grow and harvest the crops in the first place—deserve high priority.

A critical task for public policy, as articulated in country Poverty Reduction Strategies, should then be to promote concurrent investment across a range of critical sectors aimed at minimizing or eliminating the tradeoffs, and building on synergies identified earlier. Concurrent investment to alleviate the household labor constraint disproportionately affecting females will go a long way to helping to realize the benefits of investment in human development. Investing in cleaner domestic energy sources will have very important multiplier effects on achievement of both education- and health-related Millennium Development Goals. It could actually be argued that access to basic infrastructure provides double benefits by reducing the time spent on domestic chores and the fetching of wood and water, and also increasing the realm of small business opportunities and production activities made feasible thanks to water and electricity.

References

Barwell, I. 1996. *Transport and the Village: Findings from African Village-Level Travel and Transport Surveys and Related Studies*. World Bank Discussion Paper No. 344, Africa Region Series, Washington, D.C.

Berio, A.J. 1983. *Time Allocation Surveys*, Paper presented at the 11th International Congress of Anthropology Sciences, Vancouver, Canada.

Blackden, C.M., and E. Morris-Hughes. 1993. *Paradigm Postponed: Gender and Economic Adjustment in Sub-Saharan Africa*. Technical Note No. 13, Poverty and Human Resources Division, Technical Department, Africa Region, The World Bank.

Blackden, C.M., and C. Bhanu. 1999. *Gender, Growth, and Poverty Reduction*. Special Program of Assistance for Africa 1998 Status Report on Poverty, World Bank Technical Paper No. 428, Washington, D.C.

Buvinic, M., and G. Rao Gupta. 1997. "Female-Headed Households and Female-Maintained Families: Are They Worth Targeting to Reduce Poverty in Developing Countries." Economic Development and Cultural Change 45:2, 259–280.

Cleaver, K.M., and G.A. Schreiber. 1994. *Reversing the Spiral: The Population, Agriculture, Environment Nexus in Sub-Saharan Africa*. Directions in Development, World Bank.

Gelb, A. 2001. "Gender and Growth: Africa's Missed Potential." Findings No. 197, Africa Region, The World Bank, Washington, D.C. April.

Green, K. 2005. *Indoor Air Pollution, Health, Energy and The Environment in Uganda: Perspectives on the Poverty-Health-Gender-Environment Nexus*. Factsheets prepared for the Uganda Country Office of the World Bank, Kampala, Uganda, November.

Harvey, A.S., and M.E. Taylor. 2002. "Time Use." In M. Grosh and P. Glewwe, eds., *Designing Household Survey Questionnaires for Developing Countries, Lessons from 15 Years of the Living Standards Measurement Survey*. Washington, D.C.: The World Bank.

Ilahi, N. 2000. "The Intra-household Allocation of Time and Tasks: What Have We Learnt from the Empirical Literature?" Policy Research Report on Gender and Development, Working Paper Series No. 13., The World Bank, Washington, D.C.

Ironmonger, D. 1999. "An Overview of Time Use Surveys." International Seminar on Time Use Studies, Center for Development Alternatives, Ahmedabad, India.

Moser, C. 1989. "Gender Planning in the Third World: Meeting Practical and Strategic Gender Needs." *World Development* 17:1799–1825.

Malmberg-Calvo, C. 1994. "Case Study on the Role of Women in Rural Transport: Access of Women to Domestic Facilities." SSATP Working Paper No. 11, Technical Department, Africa Region, The World Bank.

Vickery, C. 1977. "The Time-Poor: A New Look at Poverty." *Journal of Human Resources* 12:27–48.

World Bank. 1999. *Tanzania: Social Sector Review*. A World Bank Country Study, Washington, D.C.

———. 2001. *Engendering Development: Through Gender Equality in Rights, Resources, and Voice*. World Bank Policy Research Report, Washington, D.C.

———. 2006. *Repositioning Nutrition as Central to Development: A Strategy for Large-Scale Action*. Directions in Development, Washington, D.C.

PART I

Reviews of the Literature

CHAPTER 2

Gender and Time Poverty in Sub-Saharan Africa

Aslihan Kes and Hema Swaminathan[4]

This paper examines the links between time use and poverty in Sub-Saharan Africa. Drawing on a broader definition of poverty to include 'time poverty,' the paper presents a conceptual framework linking both market and household work, and reviews some of the available literature and studies on time use in Sub-Saharan Africa. It presents evidence on time use for domestic tasks and care activities within the household, focusing in particular on the limited data and evidence currently available in time use surveys on care burdens in the context of HIV/AIDS. The paper concludes by stressing the importance of investing in infrastructure focused on the needs of the household economy, including water, fuel provisioning, and labor-saving technology accessible to women.

The definition of poverty has evolved significantly over time. Today, poverty is no longer viewed as solely an economic phenomenon, based on consumption or income measures alone. Poverty is seen as multidimensional, encompassing both income/consumption dimensions and other dimensions relating to human development outcomes, insecurity, vulnerability, powerlessness, and exclusion. It is also increasingly recognized that poverty, in its many dimensions, is experienced differently by men and by women, and that, consequently, gender analysis of poverty is essential for a fuller understanding of poverty dynamics and for articulating effective poverty reduction strategies.

4. The authors are with the International Center for Research on Women. The authors gratefully acknowledge financial support for this study from the World Bank. The authors also would like to thank Mark Blackden, Diane Elson, Maria Sagrario Floro, and Caren Grown for detailed and very constructive comments on previous drafts of the paper. The authors also thank Elizabeth Nicoletti for her assistance in the production of the paper.

While the relationship between gender, work, and poverty has been explored in the literature,[5] the application of a time lens to understand poverty and to inform poverty reduction strategies has not been mainstreamed in poverty analysis or strategies. This paper, along with others in this volume, aims to contribute to the wider effort to incorporate time use analysis into poverty analysis, and to draw insights from this work to inform the preparation of poverty reduction strategies. This paper examines time poverty in Sub-Saharan Africa from a gender analytical point of view and explores its implications for poverty reduction strategies. The paper is organized as follows. The next section presents a simplified conceptual framework for discussion of time use patterns and their linkages to poverty, while the section after that reviews some of the available literature on men's and women's time use in various sectors and synthesizes the principal findings from time use studies in Sub-Saharan Africa. The third section discusses some of the methodological issues relating to the conduct of time use surveys with a focus on the special requirements of time use surveys in the region. Lastly, the final section presents some key conclusions and recommendations for moving forward on the incorporation of time use analysis and time poverty into broader poverty analysis and poverty reduction strategies in Sub-Saharan Africa.

Conceptual Framework Linking Time Use and Poverty

The conceptual framework presented in this section explores the linkages between individuals' time allocation and the concept of time poverty in an agrarian developing country context (Figure 2.1). Currently, there are two main approaches used to define and measure work. One approach, codified in the System of National Accounts (SNA) as most recently revised in 1993, defines work in terms of formal and informal market work and non-market subsistence work for production of goods, and is the basis for calculating the Gross Domestic Product (GDP). This approach excludes non-market work producing services for own-consumption within the household. A more extensive discussion of what is, and is not, included in the SNA, and how non-market work is captured, is presented in the paper by Charmes in this volume (Chapter 3).

A second approach defines work and activity in a wider sense, and attempts to capture work activities and labor allocations that are not otherwise included in national accounts or economic analysis. Time use surveys are the principal instrument for capturing this wider approach. As illustrated in Figure 2.1, individuals' time use can be broadly classified as market work and non-market work. Production of goods and services for the market is grouped under market economy activities and includes both formal and informal employment, and is counted in the SNA and in calculation of GDP. The main activities that are included in the non-market, or household, economy are subsistence production, reproductive work, and volunteer work. As used here, subsistence production concerns production of goods for home use that in principle could be marketed such as food, clothing, soft furnishings,

---

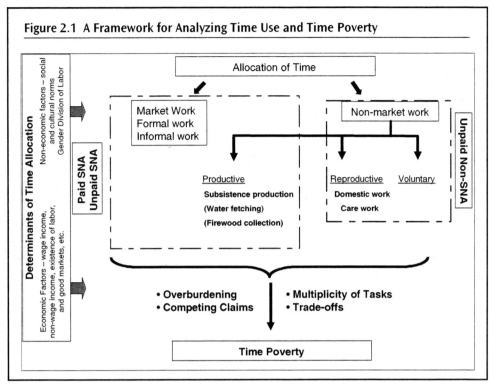

Figure 2.1 A Framework for Analyzing Time Use and Time Poverty

Source: Authors.

pottery, and housing. Reproductive work includes activities such as preparing meals, laundry, cleaning, household maintenance, and personal care. Voluntary community work comprises unpaid activity in community and civic associations such as self-help groups of mothers organizing to run a soup kitchen or to secure improvements in neighborhood safety (Elson 2002).

Evidence from various time use surveys suggests that there are marked differences in how men and women allocate their time between market and non-market work. Although some of these differences in time allocation can be explained through economic factors such as wages, non-wage income, and the functioning of labor and goods markets, in many societies economic factors are only secondary to non-economic factors in determining time use patterns (Ilahi 2000). In many settings, social and cultural norms underpin what is often a fairly rigid gender division of labor, where some tasks are strictly viewed as "men's work" and others as "women's work" (Cagatay 1998; World Bank 2001). The gender division of labor is most apparent in comparing men's and women's productive and reproductive work responsibilities. Societal norms tend to assign reproductive labor, such as looking after children, caring for the sick and the elderly, as well as preparing food, cleaning and housework, and collection of fuel and water, to women, while men are viewed as working primarily outside the domestic sphere as the main breadwinners of their households. This disproportionate allocation of female labor time to the reproductive sphere, because it is not counted in the SNA, is, in economic terms, invisible. Moreover, the fact that some labor time is allocated according to non-economic criteria that do not necessarily reflect responses to market or price signals, has implications for the smooth functioning of labor markets. These gendered patterns of labor use also mean that the capacity of individuals to reallocate their labor in response to economic incentives and to maximize productivity and efficiency, may be very limited.

The composition of the household also affects its members' time use patterns. The size of the household, the number and the gender distribution of adults, as well as the age and gender of the children, all contribute significantly to determining the options households have with respect to allocating their available labor to the full range of tasks that need to be accomplished, and to how tasks are divided among household members. Because child-care is viewed strictly as women's responsibility, the presence of young children shapes women's time use and labor market options significantly. Women who have young children tend to withdraw from the labor market or to reduce the amount of time they work outside the home (Ilahi 2000).

Similarly, the number of older children in the household, particularly girls, reduces the time women spend on various reproductive work activities. Girl children are women's main helpers in tasks such as water and fuel collection and care duties. The existence of other adult female household members also reduces the time each one must allocate to various household tasks and increases the likelihood of their involvement in wage employment (Nankhuni 2004).

The links between individuals' time use and the circumstances under which this might constitute "time poverty" have not been fully explored in the literature. Although there are frequent references to time poverty, especially for women, it is not always clear what exactly this means. More work is needed to define the concept of time poverty more precisely and to address its policy and operational implications in poverty diagnostics and poverty reduction strategies. Part II of this volume addresses this issue.

In broad terms, time poverty can be understood in the context of the burden of competing claims on individuals' time that reduce their ability to make unconstrained choices on how they allocate their time, leading, in many instances, to increased work intensity and to trade-offs among various tasks. Individuals and households at all income levels can experience time poverty as they engage in long hours of market and non-market work and have to choose between various activities. However, it can be surmised that where these tradeoffs become particularly severe, as is likely to be the case in households that are income poor, have fewer assets, and less available labor, time poverty may become a particularly important problem.

Poor households depend heavily on their members' time and labor for the provision of goods and services that are essential for their well-being and survival. When faced with severe time constraints, and lacking the economic resources to access market substitutes, these households may have to resort to making tradeoffs between activities which may directly affect their members' well-being. These may be short-term intersectoral tradeoffs as well as intergenerational tradeoffs with far reaching consequences. The negative impact of these tradeoffs can be observed in various dimensions of "human poverty" such as food security, child nutrition, health, and education. For instance, time that has to be allocated to care responsibilities may cause individuals to forego certain responsibilities in subsistence agricultural production which may adversely affect agricultural output and consequently threaten household food security and compromise child nutrition and health. Conversely, time spent on agricultural production shaped particularly around seasonal labor requirements may lead to tradeoffs in the form of less time on care and domestic work. This may impede, among other things, the timely preparation and consumption of adequate food and adversely affect household and particularly children's nutrition. Finally, household time poverty may require children to contribute time and labor to various tasks and therefore forego an education, which in turn perpetuates the intergenerational transmission of poverty, and undermines efforts to meet the Millennium Development Goals (MDGs hereafter).

Besides the links that exist between time poverty and other dimensions of human poverty, there also are several potential direct links between time and income poverty. Time poverty can exacerbate income poverty in poor households in several ways. First, low-productivity in many non-market tasks renders them time- and labor-intensive, thus reducing the availability of time to participate in more economically productive activities. Second, due to the gendered division of labor that causes poor substitutability of labor allocation in non-market work, individuals, particularly women, are unable to take full advantage of economic opportunities and participate in income-generating activities. Third, time poverty also impedes individuals' ability to expand capabilities through education and skills development, thereby enhancing economic returns in the market place.

Gender and Time Use Patterns in Sub-Saharan Africa

This section reviews some of the available data and information on time use in Sub-Saharan Africa. A more extensive treatment of data from recently conducted national time use surveys in Benin, South Africa, Madagascar, and Mauritius, as well as the time use module of the Ghana Living Measurement Survey, is presented in Chapter 3 by Charmes. The most critical drawback of the existing national level time use surveys is that they do not collect any demographic and economic information that would enable an in-depth analysis of time use patterns of men and women. Overall, the results from these surveys confirm the sharp gender division of labor between market (SNA) and household (non-SNA) activities, and that, in general, women are relatively more time poor than men, once their household economy (non-SNA) work is taken into account.

Table 2.1. Time Devoted to Economic Activity and to Work, By Gender in Benin (1998), South Africa (2000), Madagascar (2001), and Mauritius (2003) (Minutes per day)

	Benin		South Africa		Madagascar		Mauritius	
	Women	Men	Women	Men	Women	Men	Women	Men
SNA production	235	235	115	190	175	290	116	296
Non-SNA production: care and domestic activities	208	67	228	75	221	47	277	73
Total work	443	302	343	265	396	337	393	369
% SNA in total work	53.0%	77.8%	33.5%	71.7%	44.2%	86.1%	29.5%	80.2%

Source: Chapter 3.

Table 2.2. Average Time Spent in Agricultural Activities by Gender in Burkina Faso, Kenya, Nigeria, and Zambia (Minutes per day)

	Burkina Faso	Kenya	Nigeria	Zambia
Men	420	258	420	384
Women	498	372	540	456

Source: Saito and others 1994.

In Sub-Saharan Africa, both men and women engage in a number of productive and reproductive work activities. Time use studies from the region reveal that women spend more time than men at work particularly when their inputs in non-SNA production, namely domestic and care work, are included.

In Sub-Saharan Africa, children and adolescents, particularly girls, also have important economic roles in their household. In Tanzania, girls at every age have heavier work burdens than boys (Mason and Khandker in Ritchie, Lloyd, and Grant 2004). In Uganda, girls work 21.6 hours per week while boys 18.8 hours a week (Uganda DHS in Ritchie, Lloyd, and Grant 2004). A cross-country study which includes two countries from the region, South Africa and Kenya also shows that girls spend more time on non-SNA work in the form of household work compared to boys (Ritchie, Lloyd, and Grant 2004).

Gender, Time Use, and Agriculture

Agriculture is the main source of livelihood in Sub-Saharan Africa. It accounts for 35 percent of the region's GDP and 70 percent of its employment (World Bank 2000). Women provide about 50 to 75 percent of all agricultural labor in the region (Saito 1994). A study conducted by IFPRI indicates that African women undertake about 80 percent of the work in food storage and transportation, 90 percent of the work of hoeing and weeding, and 60 percent of the work in harvesting and marketing (Quisumbing et al. 1995, in Blackden and Canagarajah 2003). Women's average daily hours in agricultural work in four Sub-Saharan African countries is almost 467 minutes a day, compared with about 371 minutes a day for men (Table 2.2). An earlier study by Leplaideur (1978) in Cameroon also reveals that women spend significantly more time on agricultural tasks: they spend 348 minutes a day on production of food crops, while men spend 270 minutes a day on food and export crop production.[6]

Notwithstanding subregional variations, there is an important gender division of labor among various agricultural tasks. Women are primarily responsible for food processing, crop transportation, and weeding and hoeing, while men do most of the land clearing. Given these patterns, the effect of productivity-enhancing and time-saving

---

6. The earlier village level time use studies were designed to measure the diversity of farming work and gender division of labor. The recent time use surveys diverge from these earlier studies as they do not collect gender disaggregated time use data on various agricultural activities.

technological change is unlikely to be gender neutral. However, few empirical studies examine the impact of technical change on time allocation at the household level, and there are even fewer studies that disaggregate the impact by gender (Ilahi 2000). A study by Rubin (1990) of time use patterns of women and men in South Nyanza, Kenya explores whether changing farming technology—in the form of the introduction of a sugar cane outgrower scheme—affects women's time use patterns. The study findings suggest that women in cane producing households spend more time on domestic work and in craft work, such as basket weaving, and also have more leisure time compared with women in non-cane growing households who spend more time on food crop production, marketing, and transport, as well as in hired agricultural labor. Other studies also show that women reallocate time saved as a result of technological change in agriculture to other income-generating activities, to a variety of community and individual projects, and to domestic responsibilities (Malmberg-Calvo 1994; Blackden 2002).

Household Fuel and Water Provisioning

Although not consistently implemented by statistical agencies at the national level, since 1993 activities such as water fetching and firewood collection are counted in principle as part of SNA work. Inclusion of these activities in the SNA is important, not only because it is one way to make visible a category of work for which women are primarily responsible, but also because, as the time use data show, this represents a very substantial time and energy allocation on the part of women. This is confirmed in many data sources, including the five Sub-Saharan Africa national time use surveys presented in Charmes (see Chapter 3) and in other papers in this volume.

Fetching water and collecting firewood are also associated with child labor, though the evidence is not conclusive if boys or girls spend more time on these activities. Nankhuni (2004) studies children's time allocation on natural resource collection in Malawi and finds that being female is the most significant determinant of a child participating in natural resource collection. Her results also indicate that girls are more likely than boys to be burdened by resource collection responsibilities while simultaneously attending school.

Environmental degradation, as manifested by lack of clean water and deforestation, can significantly increase women's and girls' work burdens and total time allocated to firewood and water collection. The time and distance that women and girls need to travel to collect water increase substantially as clean water resources are exhausted. Similarly, deforestation significantly increases the time that needs to be allocated for firewood collection. A recent study by Nankhuni (2004) in Malawi suggests that women who live in areas with moderate to severe wood deficits spend more time on housework and less time on self or wage employment.

Care and Domestic Work

Reproductive tasks, such as housework, cooking, care for children, the sick, and elderly household members, are necessary to maintain families. The time required for these activities is usually positively correlated with the poverty level of households (Barnett and Whiteside 2002). Poor households in rural areas depend on female household members for the provision of reproductive tasks since they lack the economic means to access market substitutes. Additionally, whenever the household is confronted by a crisis, such as illness, the time spent on care-giving and domestic work increases significantly. Women and girls bear a large portion of these unpaid reproductive responsibilities which are often made more time consuming due to the lack of adequate household technologies. Cooking and childcare are among the most time-consuming of women's reproductive responsibilities, as revealed in the time use surveys presented in Charmes (Chapter 3) and in the other papers included in this volume.[7]

HIV-AIDS Epidemic and the Burden of Care

HIV/AIDS is a significant—and worsening—health, economic, and social issue in SSA. There are three critical factors—all interconnected—that place gender issues at the core of the HIV/AIDS pandemic in Africa, and which must be addressed systematically if the Sub-Saharan Africa is to halt the spread of AIDS. The first factor is that risk and vulnerability to HIV/AIDS are substantially different for men and for women, as is most evident in the marked age- and sex-differentiated HIV prevalence rates, and in the fact that, uniquely in Africa, women account for the majority of adults (58 percent) living with HIV/AIDS—this has implications for strategies to reduce overall prevalence in Sub-Saharan Africa and how and for whom AIDS prevention activities are undertaken. The second is that the impact of HIV/AIDS differs markedly along gender lines, reflecting men's and women's different roles and responsibilities in household and market activities, and critical gender differences in access to and control of resources—this has implications for care, support, and treatment programs, and especially for addressing the needs of the 12 million AIDS orphans in Sub-Saharan Africa. This is the critical link with the care burden and women's time use in this paper. The third is that tackling the AIDS pandemic is fundamentally about a radical change in gender relations in Sub-Saharan Africa, through behavior change that empowers both men and women to "transform" gender relations, though this dimension of the AIDS pandemic is beyond the scope of this paper.

The impact and consequences of HIV/AIDS differ markedly for men and for women, and reflect their different roles and responsibilities in household and market activities, as well as differences in their access to and control of assets and resources, as revealed in the time use data presented in this volume. What the time use data reveal, once household economy tasks are included is that the burden of care is substantial, and that it is essential, as a consequence, that any assessment of the impact of HIV/AIDS in Sub-Saharan Africa takes full account of the impact not only in the market economy, but also in the largely invisible and uncounted household economy.

The impact of the disease on patients increases incrementally, as does the burden of the disease on caretakers. The care-giving tasks resulting from having a household member affected by HIV/AIDS are numerous. Having a family member with HIV/AIDS increases the burden of other domestic activities such as housework, shopping, and transportation (Akintola 2005).

---

7. It should be noted that in many cases domestic and care work are not accurately captured in time use surveys as women don't see these activities as "work" and tend not to report them. Experience from various time use surveys reveal that these activities tend to be captured better when the questionnaire is more detailed and contextualized.

While there is qualitative evidence indicating that women are the primary caregivers at the household and community levels, the literature is surprisingly thin on the impact of serious illness on women's time allocation patterns. The few studies that have considered this with regard to HIV/AIDS are from the late 1990s, though these often do not disaggregate time allocation by individuals within the household. More recent studies have focused on understanding the impact of HIV/AIDS on various household-level welfare indicators. The lack of gender-disaggregated analysis impedes development of policies that are best suited to help HIV/AIDS-affected households.

Bollinger, Stover, and Seyoum (1999) find that, in Ethiopia, labor losses reduce the time women spend on agriculture from 33.6 hours per week for non-AIDS affected households to between 11.6 and 16.4 hours for AIDS-affected households. The study finds that the most time- consuming activity for women in HIV/AIDS-affected households is nursing at home, which amounts to 50.2 hours per week on average. The study highlights the tradeoff between women's childcare responsibilities and nursing duties. Women in non-AIDS affected households spend 25.7 hours per week caring for children while women in AIDS affected households spend between 1.9 and 13.1 hours per week on childcare.

A qualitative study of a farming region of southern Zambia finds that women were forced to abandon their agricultural work because of their care-giving responsibilities stemming from HIV/AIDS. The study concluded that the rigid division of labor in that environment was a limiting factor in household responsiveness (Waller 1997). Care-giving responsibilities can also have intergenerational impacts as found by Yamano and Jayne (2004) in rural Kenya. In their study of working age adult mortality and primary school attendance, the authors find that adult mortality negatively affects children's, in particularly girls', schooling even in the period directly before mortality, most likely because the children are sharing in the burden of care-giving (Yamano and Jayne in Gillespie and Kadiyala 2005). Hansen and others (1994) study four home care programs in Zimbabwe and estimate the cost incurred by households in caring for a bedridden patient for three months. The study concludes that the time spent on caring, diverted from other activities such as food production, employment, education and care of other household members, is the highest cost burden incurred by these households. In Kagabiro, Tanzania, the labor loss of households affected by HIV/AIDS is on average 43 percent (Tibaijuka 1997).

Challenges to Reducing Women's Time Poverty

As the sectoral breakdown of time use among genders in Sub-Saharan Africa reveals, there are marked differences in how much and on which tasks men and women spend their time. Women's tasks are often made more difficult because of inadequate infrastructure for water, energy, and transport, as well as women's lack of access to productivity-enhancing technology that is responsive to their specific needs and work burdens.

The lack of adequate infrastructure, such as feeder roads, water and sanitation systems, and energy sources, as well as the under-provision of services flowing from these systems, imposes greater work burdens on women and lengthens the time it takes to perform activities related to household survival and economic production (see Box 2.1).

A 1995 UNDP Report analyzes rural "total transport demand" in the region (all movement of people and goods by any means, including women headloading water, pack animals moving relief supplies, and non-motorized vehicles on footpaths and trails).

Box 2.1: Time Can be Saved through Better Infrastructure: Examples from Uganda and Zambia

A study conducted in Mbale, Eastern Uganda and Kasama, Zambia illustrates the time saving effects of better infrastructure: If woodlots were within 30 minutes of the homestead and if the water source were within 400 meters, Mbale households, specifically women and girls, would save more than 900 hours/year; around 240 hours in firewood collection and 660 hours in water collection. Similarly, in Kasama, Zambia they would save 125 to 664 hours a year in water collection and 119 to 610 hours a year in firewood collection.

Source: Barwell 1996.

It finds that total transport requirements in agricultural production and to meet essential domestic needs (water and fuel collection for example) are much more significant there than those of crop marketing. This burden largely falls on women, who expend 70 percent of the time and over 80 percent of the effort devoted to these tasks (Urasa in UNDP 1995). Similarly, Malmberg-Calvo (1994) in her study of three Sub-Saharan African countries (Ghana, Tanzania, and Zambia) finds that women account for about 65 percent of the time spent on all transport activities in the rural household, and about 71 to 96 percent of the time spent on domestic travel activities. While men's main transport contributions are in association with crop establishment, weeding and transport of harvested crops, women are active in both of these tasks, as well as in transport work associated with basic needs provisioning and crop marketing (Bryceson and Howe 1993).

Improving women's access to alternative sources of energy other than traditional biofuels can reduce not only their time burdens, but also their exposure to indoor air pollution and other risks to their health. Cooking fuels such as kerosene and liquefied petroleum gas (LPG) are good substitutes for traditional biofuels because of their higher thermal efficiency and relative lack of pollutants. The use of such fuels also saves women time for more productive activities by eliminating the need to walk long distances to gather fuel, and by reducing cooking time. As shown in a study of India, time thus saved can be used for income-earning pursuits, attention to children, civic participation, or leisure (Barnes and Sen 2003).

Strengthening transitional, low-cost solutions that are already being used by the poor can also reduce women's time and effort burdens (Modi 2004). These include diesel-powered minigrids for charging batteries that can be carried to households and multifunctional platforms powered by a diesel engine for low-cost rural motive power. The multifunctional platform, implemented in Mali, has been particularly successful (see Box 2.2).

Improvements in the form of labor-saving and productivity-improving technologies in agriculture can significantly increase productivity, reduce the number of hours worked, and relieve individuals' time poverty (see Box 2.3; Von Braun, Swaminathan, and Rosegrant 2005). The amount of time and energy women spend on agricultural tasks such as harvesting, weeding, hoeing, planting, and food processing can be reduced considerably with the help of adequate inputs such as improved seeds, fertilizers, and pesticides in addition to labor-saving tools and equipment. As the time they need to spend on agricultural tasks is reduced, women can allocate their time to other work, including work in the nonagricultural sector.

**Box 2.2: Diesel-powered Multifunctional Platforms Reduce the Burdens
on Women in Mali**

By many measures Mali is one of the poorest and least developed countries in the world. Nearly three-quarters of its roughly 12 million people live in semi-arid rural areas, where poverty is most severe. Electrification is virtually nonexistent, and most of the country's energy supply, particularly in rural areas, comes from biomass. Women and girls are responsible for the time-consuming and labor-intensive work of fuel collection.

Beginning in 1993 the UN Industrial Development Organization and the International Fund for Agricultural Development initiated a program to decrease the burden of fuel collection by supplying labor-saving energy services and promoting the empowerment of women by supplying multifunctional platforms to rural villages. The multifunctional platform is a 10-horsepower diesel engine with modular components that can supply motive power for time- and labor-intensive work such as agricultural processing (milling, de-husking) and electricity for lighting (approximately 200–250 small bulbs), welding, or pumping water. Between 1999 and 2004, 400 platforms were installed, reaching about 8,000 women in villages across the country.

Although the benefits are shared by many in the villages, women's organizations own, manage, and control the platform. Capacity building and institutional support by the project, strong in the early phases, taper off, leaving the women's groups in charge of platform operation, relying on a network of private suppliers, technicians, and partners. The women's groups cover 40–60 percent of initial cost. The remaining costs are covered by international donors and local partners (nongovernmental organizations, social clubs, and other donors).

A study of 12 villages found several beneficial impacts:

- The platforms reduced the time required for labor-intensive tasks from many hours to a matter of minutes. The time and labor women saved was shifted to income-generating activities, leading to an average daily increase in women's income of $0.47. Rice production and consumption also increased, an indirect benefit arising from time saved.

- The ratios of girls to boys in schools and the proportion of children reaching grade 5 improved, as young girls were needed less for time-consuming chores.

- Increases in time and the mother's socioeconomic status accompanying the introduction of the platforms correlate with improvements in women's health and increases in the frequency of women's visits to local clinics for prenatal care.

Overall, the program in Mali offers compelling evidence that time saved in the lives of women and children, combined with the added socioeconomic benefits to women's groups of controlling and managing the platform as a resource, can yield substantial benefits to health and welfare.

Source: Fraccia and others in Modi 2004.

Box 2.3: Manual Versus Mechanized Food Processing

In Nigeria, threshing and milling of grains before pounding may take 2 to 3 hours each day. 82 women hours are needed to process one drum of oil palm fruits. Cassava processing without a grating machine can take two days of a week. Grinders that can grate a basin of cassava in one minute compared to two hours by hand are estimated to be present in only 5 percent of Imo State Villages.

Studies carried out in Africa show that it may take up to 13 hours just to pound enough maize to feed a family for 4 to 5 days.

In the Congo, processing of tapioca and maize took four times as long as all the work hours spent on the cultivation of these crops.

Source: Ay in Saito and others 1994; Rogers in Blackden 2002.

Box 2.4: Women's Adoption of Appropriate Food Processing Technologies in Tanzania

---

Most households in Tanzania use traditional sun drying methods. Women's time is the only required input. Foods are placed on mats or the bare ground and exposed to direct sunlight. Unfortunately, the preserved foods often become contaminated and lose their nutritional value. To improve the food drying process, the Tanzania Food and Nutrition Centre (TFNC) with colleagues in the Ministry of Agriculture and the Ministry of Community Development, Children and Women's Affairs developed improved solar dyers to reduce foods' exposure to contaminants and direct sun, and the time needed for drying. The quality of food produced through these driers was more consistent and the nutritional content improved.

The program developed models that responded to women's needs through providing individual portable driers. This saved considerable time and also provided substantial flexibility for women. The program also included an education strategy that ensured all community members received the same basic information on this new technology.

Over the course of the study, the proportion of women in intervention and control communities who reported drying vegetables changed somewhat between baseline (88 and 94 percent) and the next project later (99 and 98 percent). However, adopters produced on average 55 liters after one year as compared to only 33 liters for non-adopters in the intervention communities. Adopters also dried significantly larger quantities of a variety of vegetables that were cultivated in home gardens than did non-adopters. Moreover, the project had the effect of increasing the consumption of vitamin A and provitamin A rich foods among children whose mothers' adopted the improved solar as opposed to children whose mothers were non-adopters.

Source: Mulokozi and others 2000.

In many cases, compared with men, women's access to time-saving and productivity-enhancing inputs and technologies is very limited. Although this may be linked to a certain extent to the lack of adequate technologies directly applicable to some of these tasks, in most cases the technology is available but out of reach of women. Programs aimed at introducing productivity-enhancing techniques need to identify the community specific causes of why women are unable to access these technologies and subsequently address these in their design to make sure women benefit equally from their interventions (see Box 2.4).

Methodologies Used in Time Use Surveys

In developed countries, time use surveys have had a long history. The surveys are used to complement the official statistics, which already give a fairly accurate account of market activities, by providing additional information on time spent on activities such as household work, childcare, and leisure. However, in Sub-Saharan Africa, as noted above, a significant amount of productive activity takes place within the household that is not fully captured by official statistics. The design, methodology, and implementation of time use surveys in Sub-Saharan Africa require special attention to the region's circumstances. In this region, most of the respondents of time use surveys are likely to be illiterate necessitating use of illustrated survey materials or interviewer-administered surveys. Similarly, respondents seldom own or wear watches, lack a modern concept of time, and relate their activities to fluctuations of nature such as day time or the season (Harvey and Taylor 2000). To overcome this problem, special tools need to be used to translate local perception of time into a standard 24 hour timetable. Also, in most countries in the region, people have overlapping work responsibilities that involve tradeoffs with implications for survival and growth. This is particularly evident in women's time use patterns because their time is already stretched to the limit, and therefore, they are forced to undertake simultaneous responsibilities.

Women often do not consider domestic and personal care activities as work, and hence, do not report it (Harvey and Taylor 2000). The omission of such activities may in turn cause a downward bias in the measurement of intensity of women's work. Time use surveys need to be designed to capture individuals' work intensity and the tradeoffs they face. Finally, agriculture is the dominant sector in Sub-Saharan Africa and there are distinct seasonal variations in the workloads of women and men. Therefore, it is important to undertake the surveys over a year at different points in time to capture the impact of seasonality.

Certain tradeoffs need to be considered in deciding the type and scope of surveys. A large-scale time use survey, more likely to be conducted by major statistical agencies, can reveal patterns of time use by different demographic groups as well as those in different socio-economic clusters but would be costly to implement. Small-scale studies, although not as detailed and representative, are important in drawing attention to the need for larger studies. Qualitative studies of time use are very useful since they provide in-depth information on the sociocultural conditions that determine time use patterns of individuals within a household. However, they should not be treated as a substitute for quantitative analysis; rather a combination of both qualitative and quantitative information is desirable in developing policies and interventions.

Various methodologies have been followed in conducting time use surveys.[8] In developing countries, direct observation has been one of the preferred methods for conducting time use surveys. This method addresses the issues of illiteracy and time measurement since it uses an outside observer to record the activities of the subjects he or she follows during the day. It is also helpful in capturing activities that are unstructured and where simultaneous tasks are performed. There are, however, some drawbacks to this method. First of all, it is highly costly and forces the selection of a smaller sample size. Also knowing that they are being observed, people tend to change their pattern of behavior. Finally, the observer may find it difficult to distinguish between market and non-market activities. Due to the drawbacks of this method others have been explored as well.

Interviewer administered time diaries provide a chronological report of the time studied, provide consistency in time activity data, and forces full accounting. Depending on the design, this method may allow for recording of both primary and concurrent activities. The disadvantage of this method is that the design may become too complicated to implement, especially in developing countries, where interviewers and respondents have low levels of education (Harvey and Taylor 2000).

---

8. A list of methods used in time use surveys including the advantages and disadvantages of each of these methods are provided in Annex 3.

Box 2.5: Valuing Unpaid Non-SNA Work

Valuing unpaid work is important in capturing the economic contribution of unpaid non-SNA work. Unpaid work and particularly unpaid care work yield significant positive externalities to the economy that remain unnoticed unless they are quantified in monetary terms (Budlender 2002). There are several approaches to value unpaid work. These approaches can be grouped into four broad categories: the mean wage approach, the opportunity cost approach, the generalist approach, and the specialist approach. The mean wage approach calculates the average wage in the economy as a whole and assigns this wage to unpaid non-SNA work. The average is usually calculated separately for men and women and assigned accordingly. The opportunity cost approach uses the market wage rate foregone by doing unpaid non-SNA work as the wage rate. The generalist approach takes as wage rate the average wage of home helpers meanwhile the specialist approach assumes that different people with different qualifications would take over different household tasks and uses their wage rates to calculate the wage rate for housework.

Source: Budlender 2002; Swiebel 1999.

Conclusions and Recommendations

This paper has sought to bring to light a critical gender-relevant dimension of poverty in Sub-Saharan Africa: time poverty. Its aim has been to inform the analysis of poverty in Sub-Saharan Africa in a manner that in turn can inform policy and operational priorities. Time poverty, while not a new concept, adds important insights to the understanding of poverty dynamics in Sub-Saharan Africa, how these dynamics affect men and women differently, and how they might be acted on in poverty reduction strategies. Time use data in Sub-Saharan Africa, as shown in the literature review in this paper, and in other papers in this volume, perform some very important functions. They reveal the co-existence of both market and household economies, and how they are interdependent. They show not only the sheer size and significance of the household economy, measured in terms of the amount of time spent on household economy tasks, but also the disproportionate burden that falls on women for the accomplishment of these tasks, a burden that has been greatly exacerbated by the HIV/AIDS pandemic. They show that there are important synergies, and critical tradeoffs between and among tasks in these economies, with important implications for poverty reduction and development outcomes. Understanding the time impact of development interventions becomes a critical dimension of appraisal and evaluation.

What the time data show us is that there are important differences in gender roles, which constitute a major obstacle to development and poverty reduction in Sub-Saharan Africa. Women's significant, though understated, roles in economic production (agriculture and the informal sector, predominantly) and their pivotal position in household management and welfare (food preparation, health and hygiene, childcare, and education) are central to Sub-Saharan Africa's economic development and social survival. Time use data confirm the evidence available in the agricultural sector showing that women are indeed the continent's principal food producers and have primary responsibility for assuring food availability in the family: they are therefore central to the attainment of

---

Box 2.6: Making Extension Services Tailored to Women's Needs

Extension services are an important means of disseminating information on new techniques, seed varieties, marketing, and related services in agriculture. PRSPs such as the Ugandan PEAP acknowledge the importance of these services in improving productivity in agriculture. Although few studies investigate the direct links between access to agricultural extension and time use, by improving productivity, these services can reduce the drudgery and time involved in key agricultural tasks undertaken by women. Gender-sensitive training is often required for extension workers, and the content of extension services should be structured to include resources, commodities, and tasks that are more relevant to women's crops and agricultural roles. Extension workers need to specifically target women farmers by moving away from their traditional audience of household heads. Finally, services should be designed to reach women who are constrained by lack of time and, in certain communities, limited mobility.

Source: Saito and others 1994.

Sub-Saharan Africa's food security goals and to meeting family nutritional needs. Women are the principal gatherers and users of wood for fuel and water for washing and cooking: how they do this critically affects the pace and extent of environmental degradation and the fertility of the soil. Women have primary responsibility for child rearing and family health: on this the future productivity of the country's human resource base depends.

Time use data show that both men and women have multiple roles and responsibilities. What particularly characterizes women's roles, in contrast to those of men, is that they must carry out their roles simultaneously, not sequentially. This is evident not only in the extent of women's labor burden and the very long working hours, but also in the harsh choices and tradeoffs that women inevitably have to make because of the simultaneous competing claims on their time. Addressing time poverty in a way that speaks to these gendered differences therefore needs to be integral to strengthening poverty reduction strategies (PRSs).

As the analysis in this paper also demonstrates, there exist a strong correlation between gendered differences in time poverty and men and women's roles in various sectors. The identification in PRSPs of this relationship with particular attention to gender roles in various sectors is instrumental in devising interventions that can target reductions in time poverty (see Box 2.6).

Time use analysis can strengthen the policies in sectors that are identified as key to reducing poverty and improving living and working conditions of women, including agricultural modernization and commercialization, infrastructure, and employment, among others. Such analysis can also provide guidance in prioritizing sectoral allocation of public expenditures. Time use analysis could support this by being an essential component of the monitoring and evaluation of the policies and interventions proposed under PRSPs (see Box 2.7).

Analysis of time use data reveals the significance of the household economy. This in turn suggests that an important priority for poverty reduction strategies is to invest in this economy. Such investment would aim to reduce the "household time overhead," and relieve the time burdens on women. It would have the added benefit of specifically

---

Box 2.7: Using Time Use Data in Project Evaluations

A review of transport projects supported by the World Bank found that in 2002 four percent of these projects included a gender component or gender actions, compared with 15 percent of water supply projects and 35 percent of agriculture projects. Among those World Bank financed transport programs that pay attention to gender, two are worth mentioning. The Shova Kalula bicycle project in South Africa aimed at providing low cost mobility solutions such as non-motorized transport. The project diagnostic incorporated some time use data on time spent by workers and students on transport. A review of the project found that it significantly reduced the amount of time students spend traveling to school. There was also case study evidence that women widely used bicycles to access the market to "buy and sell vegetables" (Mahapa 2003). The gender review of the Mubende Fort Portal Trunk Road Rehabilitation project in the Ugandan road sector program also noted the effects of the rehabilitation project on women's travel time to markets, trading opportunities, farm inputs, and so forth. (Tanzarn 2003). Making time use analysis part of project evaluations such as the ones mentioned above can potentially improve their impact and provide better guidance in designing future interventions.

---

reducing the tradeoffs among competing uses of scarce labor. Examples of such investment priorities include infrastructure to provide clean and accessible water supply, and energy focused on domestic requirements (notably for cooking fuel). Labor-saving domestic technology relating to food processing has the potential to raise women's labor productivity and save time. Transport interventions can be oriented to reflect the different needs of men and women, so as to improve women's access to transport services (including intermediate means of transport), commensurate with their load-carrying responsibilities. Energy policy and investment priorities need to focus on alternative energy sources, and to address the domestic energy needs of households. This will have important multiplier effects on improving health, saving time, and enabling girls to go to (and stay) in school.

Of particular importance in Sub-Saharan Africa is the need to address the huge care burdens facing women in the face of HIV/AIDS, given their disproportionate responsibilities in this area.

As discussed earlier, care for AIDS sufferers occurs in households alongside the other caring work that women do to sustain their families. As the epidemic progresses, the burden of caring for those living with HIV and AIDS can overtake and displace not only the other crucial work of the care economy, but also the ability of women to perform their critical economic functions in agriculture and food security.

In recent years international and national level policymakers have begun to recognize the need for a more coherent, expansive, and inclusive "care agenda" for HIV/AIDS, and that systems need to be put into place to help households and communities provide care for those who are sick and dying from AIDS (Ogden, Esim, and Grown 2004). Although many community-based health care programs are in place, there is an urgent need for these programs to take account of the time burdens of women, to avoid adding to these burdens, and to be more strongly integrated with wider family care and production work carried out by women.

References

Akintola, O. 2005. "Unpaid HIV/AIDS Care in Southern Africa: Nature, Contexts and Implications." Presented at Global Conference on Unpaid Work and the Economy: Gender, Poverty, and the Millennium Development Goals, October 1–3, Bard College, Annandale-On-Hudson, NY. UNDP and Levy Economics Institute Bureau for Development Policy.

Apps, P. 2002. "Gender, Time Use, and Models of the Household." Sydney: Faculty of Law, University of Sydney.

Ay, P. 1990. *Women in Food Processing: Traditional Palm Oil Production and Changes through the Introduction of Appropriate Technology.* Ibadan: UNDP/ILO/FDARD and Book Builders Ltd.

Bamberger, M., M. Blackden, L. Fort, and V. Manoukian. 2000. "Chapter 10: Gender" In *PRSP Sourcebook*. Washington, D.C., The World Bank.

Barnes, D., and M. Sen. 2003. "The Impact of Energy on Women's Lives in Rural India." Washington, D.C.: UNDP/World Bank Energy Sector Management Assistance Programme.

Barnett, T., and A. Whiteside. 2002. "Poverty and HIV/AIDS: Impact, Coping, and Mitigation Policy." In *AIDS, Public Policy and Child Well-being*. Florence, Italy: UNICEF-IRC.

Barwell, I. 1996. *Transport and the Village*. World Bank Discussion Paper 344. Washington, D.C.: The World Bank.

Bhargava, A. 1997. "Nutritional Status and the Allocation of Time in Rwandese Households." *Journal of Econometrics* 77:277–295.

Blackden, C.M. 2002. "All Work and No Time: Time Poverty as a Development Issue in Africa." Poverty Reduction and Economic Management, Africa Region, The World Bank, Washington, D.C. Processed.

Blackden, C.M., and R.S. Canagarajah. 2003. "Gender and Growth in Africa: Evidence and Issues." Presented at UNECA Expert Meeting on Pro-Poor Growth, June 23–24, Kampala, Uganda.

Bollinger, L., J. Stover, and E. Seyoum. 1999. "The Economic Impact of AIDS in Ethiopia." The POLICY Project: The Futures Group International in collaboration with Research Triangle Institute (RTI), Centre for Development and Population Activities (CEDPA).

Bryceson, D.F., and J. Howe. 1993. "Rural household transport in Africa: Reducing the burden on women?" *World Development* 21(11):1715–1728.

Budlender, D. 2002. "Why Should We Care about Unpaid Care Work?" A guidebook prepared for the UNIFEM Southern African Region Office, Harare, Zimbabwe. Cape Town: Community Agency for Social Enquiry.

Cagatay, N. 1998. "Engendering Macroeconomics and Macroeconomic Policies." New York: United Nations Development Programme (UNDP), Social Development & Poverty Elimination Division, Bureau for Development Policy.

Canagarajah, S., and H. Coulombe. 1998. "Child Labor and Schooling in Ghana." World Bank Policy Research Working Paper No. 1844. Washington, D.C.: The World Bank.

Charmes, J. 2005. "A Review of Empirical Evidence on Time Use in Africa from UN-sponsored Surveys." (Chapter 3 of this volume.)

Chen, M., J. Vanek, F. Lund, J. Heintz with R. Jhabvala and C. Bonner. 2005. *Progress of the World's Women 2005*. New York: United Nations Development Fund for Women (UNIFEM).

Elson, D. 2002. "Macroeconomics and Macroeconomics Policy from a Gender Perspective." Presented at Public Hearing of Study Commission, "Globalisation of the World Economy—Challenges and Responses," February 18, Deutscher Bundestag.

Floro, M.S. 1995. "Women's Well-Being, Poverty, and Work Intensity." *Feminist Economics* 1(3):1–25.

Fraccia, S., R. Lang, and B. Anderson. 2004. *Malawi Case Study*. School of International and Public Affairs, Columbia University.

Ghana Statistical Service. 1999. "Ghana Living Standards Survey Round Four (GLSS 4) 1998/99." Data User's Guide. Accra, Ghana.

Gillespie, S., and S. Kadiyala. 2005. *HIV/AIDS and Food and Nutrition Security: From Evidence to Action*. Washington, D.C.: International Food Policy Research Institute.

Goodin, R.E., M. Bittman, and P. Saunders. 2001. "If Time is Money, What is Poverty?" Presented at RC19 Conference, September, Orviedo, Spain.

Grown, C., G. Rao Gupta, and A. Kes. 2005. *Taking Action: Achieving Gender Equality and Empowering Women*. London: Earthscan.

Hansen, K., and others. 1994. "The Costs of Hospital Care at Government Health Facilities in Zimbabwe with Special Emphasis on HIV/AIDS Patients." Harare, Zimbabwe: Blair Research Institute, Ministry of Health and Family Welfare.

Haraldsen, G. 1999. "The Design of Time Use Surveys in Developed and Developing Countries." Presented at 1999 IATUR Conference, October 6–8, University of Essex, Colchester, UK.

Harvey, A.S., and M.E. Taylor. 2000. "Time Use" In Margaret Grosh and Paul Glewwe (eds.), *Designing Household Survey Questionaires: Lessons from Fifteen Years of the Living Standards Measurement Study*. Washington, D.C.: The World Bank.

Ilahi, N. 2000. "The Intra-household Allocation of Time and Tasks: What Have We Learnt from the Empirical Literature?" Policy Research Report on Gender and Development, Working Paper Series No. 13. Washington, D.C.: World Bank Development Research Group.

INSAE/PNUD. 1998. *Enquete emploi du temps au Benin, Methodologie et resultats*. Cotonou.

INSTAT. 2002. "EPM 2001. Module Emploi du Temps." Antananarivo, INSTAT-DSM/PNUD-MAG/97/007.

Leplaideur, A. 1978. *Les travauz agricoles chez les paysans du Centre-Sud Cameroun, les techniques utilisees et les temps necessaires*. Paris: IRAT.

Mahapa, S. 2003. "Integrating Gender into World Bank Financed Programs." South Africa Shova Kalula Case Study. Washington, D.C.: The World Bank.

Malmberg-Calvo, C. 1994. "Case Study on the Role of Women in Rural Transport: Access of Women to Domestic Facilities." SSATP (Sub-Saharan Africa Transport Policy Program, World Bank and Economic Commission for Africa) Working Paper No. 11. Environmentally Sustainable Development Division, Technical Department, Africa Region, The World Bank. Washington, D.C.

Mammen, K., and C. Paxson. 2000. "Women's Work and Economic Development." *Journal of Economic Perspectives* 14(4):141–164.

Mason, A.D., and S.R. Khandker. 1997. "Household Schooling Decisions in Tanzania." Washington, D.C.: The World Bank.

Modi, V. 2004. "Energy and Transport for the Poor." Paper commissioned for the U.N. Millennium Project Task Force 1. New York: Earth Institute and Columbia University, Department of Mechanical Engineering.

Mulokozi, G. and others. 2000. *Improved Solar Drying of Vitamin A-rich Foods by Women's Groups in the Singida District of Tanzania.*

Nankhuni, F. 2004. "Environmental Degradation, Resource Scarcity and Children's Welfare in Malawi: School Attendance, School Porgress, and Children's Health." In *Agricultural Economics and Demography*. University Park: The Pennsylvania State University.

Ogden, J., S. Esim, and C. Grown. 2004. "Expanding the Care Continuum for HIV/AIDS: Bringing Carers into Focus." In *Horizons Report*. Washington, D.C.: Population Council and International Center for Research on Women.

Quisumbing, A., L. R. Brown, H. Sims Feldstein, L. Haddad, and C. Pena. 1995. *Women: The Key to Food Security*. Food Policy Report. International Food Policy Research Institute: Washington, D.C.

Republic of Mauritius, Central Statistics Office. 2004. *Continuous Multi-Purpose Household Survey 2003, Main Results of the Time Use Study*. Port-Louis.

Ritchie, A., C.B. Lloyd, and M. Grant. 2004. "Gender Differences in Time Use Among Adolescents in Developing Countries: Implications of Rising School Enrollment Rates." Policy Research Division Working Paper No. 193. New York: Population Council, Inc.

Rogers, B. 1980. *The Domestication of Women: Discrimination in Developing Societies.* New York: St. Martin's Press

Rubin, D.S. 1990. "Women's Work and Children's Nutrition in South-Western Kenya." *Food & Nutrition Bulletin* 12(4).

Saito, K.A., with contributions from H. Mekonnen and D. Spurling. 1994. "Raising the Productivity of Women Farmers in Sub-Saharan Africa." Washington, D.C.: The World Bank.

SNA (System of National Accounts). 1993. "Commission of the European Communities, IMF, OECD, UN, WB."

Statistics South Africa. 2001. *A Survey of Time Use. How South African Women and Men Spend Their Time*. Pretoria.

Swiebel, J. 1999. "Unpaid Work and Policy-Making: Towards a Broader Perspective of Work and Employment." DESA Discussion Paper No. 4. New York: United Nations.

Tanzarn, N. 2003. "Integrating Gender into World Bank Financed Transport Programs" Uganda Road Sector Program Support (RSPS) Case Study. Washington, D.C.: The World Bank.

Tibaijuka, A.K. 1997. "AIDS and Economic Welfare in Peasant Agriculture: Case Studies from Kagabiro village, Kagera region, Tanzania." *World Development* 25(6):963–975.

UNDP (United Nations Development Programme). 1995. *Energy After Rio: Prospects and Challenges.*

UNESCAP (United Nations Economic and Social Commission for Asia and the Pacific). 2003. *Integrating Unpaid Work into National Policies*. Bangkok: United Nations

UNFPA (United Nations Population Fund). 2002. "State of the World Population."

Urasa, I. 1990. *Women and Rural Transport: An Assessment of their Role in Sub-Saharan Africa*. Geneva: International Labour Office (ILO).

Von Braun, J., M.S. Swaminathan, and M.W. Rosegrant. 2005. *Agriculture, Food Security, Nutrition and the MDGs*. Washington, D.C.: International Food Policy Research Institute.

Waller, K. 1997. "The Impact of HIV/AIDS on Farming Households in the Monze District of Zambia." University of Bath, UK: Centre of Development Studies.

Whitehead, A. 2003. "Failing Women, Sustaining Poverty: Gender in Poverty Reduction Strategy Papers." Report for the UK Gender and Development Network.

World Bank. 1999. "Africa Region Findings: Gender, Growth, and Poverty Reduction." Washington, D.C.: The World Bank. www.worldbank.org/afr/findings/english/find129.htm

———. 2000. *Can Africa Claim the 21st Century?* Washington, D.C.

———. 2001. *Engendering Development through Gender Equality in Rights, Resources and Voice*. Policy Research Report. Washington, D.C.

———. 2005. *Gender and Energy in Uganda: A Brief Summary of Issues for the PEAP Revision*. Washington, D.C.

Yamano, T., and T.S. Jayne. 2004. "Working-Age Adult Mortality and Primary School Attendance in Rural Kenya." *Policy Synthesis: Tegemeo Institute for Agricultural Development and Policy* (4).

Appendix Table 2.A1. Inventory and Design Components of All Cross Section and Panel Time Use Data Sources in Sub-Saharan African Countries

Country	Survey	Sample Size	Type of Survey	Survey Instrument	Mode of Data Collection
Benin	Time use survey, 1998	1787 households, 5834 respondents in rural; 1419 households, 6770 respondents in urban; ages 6–65	Module of survey on labor, income, and social indicators.	Simplified diary; 63 activities, 15 minute intervals	Face to face recall interview; one diary day
Botswana	Rural income distribution survey, 1981			Survey	
Botswana	1984				
Cameroon	1984				
Cote D'Ivoire	1982	880 women		Interview	
Cote d'Ivoire	CILSS 1985–1988	1588 households in CILSS85, 1600 households in CILSS86,87,88; ages 7 and older	Module in living standards survey	Stylized activity list; seven day recall	Face to face recall interview
Ghana	Ghana (1991–92, 1998–99)	5998 households 25664 individuals, ages 7 and older	Time use short and incomplete module in a continuous living standards measurement survey	Seven day recall; ad hoc classification.	Face to face recall interview
Kenya	1985	115 households		Participant observation	
Kenya	1990	44 women		Participant observation; open ended interview	
Kenya	1998			Interview	
Madagascar	2001	2663 households, 7743 individuals; ages 6 to 65.	Specific survey attached to a permanent survey (parallel sample)	Prelisting of 77 activities classified SNA/non SNA	Pre-listed Diary 24 hours past day
Malawi	Time allocation of adults; time allocation of children ages 7 through 11; 1995	404 households	Module of Financial Markets and Household Food Security Survey	Two day recall	

(continued)

Appendix Table 2.A1. Inventory and Design Components of All Cross Section and Panel Time Use Data Sources in Sub-Saharan African Countries (*Continued*)

Country	Survey	Sample Size	Type of Survey	Survey Instrument	Mode of Data Collection
Malawi	Adolescents ages 15 through 21; 2004	1000 adolescents	Subsection in the Malawi Diffusion and Ideation Change Project (MDICP). Ongoing longitudinal study.	Diary	
Malawi			Module of Integrated household survey		Face to face recall interview; one diary day
Mauritius	Time use survey, 2003	6480 households; 19907 individuals; ages 10 and older.	Module of continuous multipurpose household survey	Twenty four hour diary; 30 minute intervals; UN classification	
Nigeria	1982	69 households		Interview	
Nigeria	1992	429 households		Participant observation	
Nigeria	Time use in Nigeria, 1998	20 households from 4 states and Lagos; 243 respondents; 10 years and older.	Independent (pilot)	Open diary with chronological recording of activities starting; starting and ending times are recorded; total number of minutes per activity is also recorded.	Self reporting and face to face interview; one diary day.
Senegal	1983	139 mothers and children		Spot observation	
South Africa	National time use survey, 2000	8564 households; 14553 respondents; ages 10 and older.	Independent	Full diary; 30 minute intervals	Face to face recall interview; one diary day
Uganda	ULSS, 1992		Module in national integrated household survey	Stylized activity list; seven day recall	Face to face recall interview
Uganda	1993	9929 households			
Zimbabwe	1991	132 households		Interview direct measure	
Zimbabwe	1992	331 households			

Source: Budlender 2002; UNESCAP 2003.

Table 2.A2. Matrix of Empirical Studies with Data Sources, Methodology, and Outcomes

Study and Location	Data Sources	Sample and Design	Objectives	Findings
Bollinger, Stover, and Seyoum (1999) Ethopia	Household survey	100 households	Differences in workload of women in HIV/AIDS affected households versus in unaffected women.	The mean hours women spend on agricultural tasks varies between 11.6 and 16.4 in affected households compared to 33.6 hours in unaffected households. Women in affected households spend between 1.9 and 13.1 hours a week on childcare compared to 25.7 hours in unaffected households.
Canagarajah and Coulombe (1993) Ghana	Ghana Living Standards Survey (GLSS) 87/88, 88/89, 91/92, and ILO Child Labor Survey (1996)	2876 children in GLSS1, 3011 children in GLSS2, and 3859 children in GLSS3	Identify patterns explaining the prevalence of child labor in certain households	When household chores are included in the definition of work: Girls are more likely to work. The presence of children younger than 6 increases the probability of working and not attending school. Presence of female adults increases probability of schooling and not working.
Rubin Kenya		75 households interviewed over a 12 month period.	How do time use patterns between men and women differ? How did the introduction of sugar cane outgrower scheme change the patterns of time use?	Women allocate most of their time on the daily performance of household duties as well as food crop farming. Women in cane households spend more time on domestic work and in craft work. They also had more leisure time Women in non-sugar households spent more time on food crop production, marketing and transport as well as in hired agricultural labor.

(continued)

Table 2.A2. Matrix of Empirical Studies with Data Sources, Methodology, and Outcomes (*Continued*)

Study and Location	Data Sources	Sample and Design	Objectives	Findings
Yamano, Jayne Kenya	1997, 2000, 2002 panel of 1422 households	Children ages 7–14	Does working age adult mortality affect children's primary school attendance	The authors first establish that a high proportion of working age adult mortality in the household data is AIDS related. In poor households (measured in terms of asset distribution) children's school attendance is adversely affected by the death of working age adults. The probability that girls from relatively poor households attend school in the one to two year period before the death of an adult declines from 90 percent to 62 percent. One of the conclusions the authors derive is that children especially girls are sharing the burden of caring for sick working age adults
Nankhuni (2004) Malawi	Malawi Integrated Household Survey (IHS) 1997/98	10,698 households – 46,128 individuals.	Is the time children spend collecting fuel wood and water a determinant of their school attendance?	Being female is the most significant determinant of a child participating in natural resource collection. Girls are more likely to attend school while burdened by resource collection responsibilities.
Bhargava Rwanda	1982–83 longitudinal study	110 households		Substitution between women's agricultural work and their housework. Men's housework is insignificant.
Ritchie, Lloyd, and Grant Multiple countries including South Africa and Kenya from SSA	South Africa (1999); Kenya (1996); Pakistan (2001–02), India (2003), Guatemala LSMS (2000), Nicaragua LSMS (1998)	16,045 adolescents in Guatemala, 6, 148 in India, 774 in Kenya, 5,115 in Nicaragua, 8,062 in Pakistan, 3051 in South Africa	How does time use change during the transition to adulthood, does gender role differentiation intensify during the transition, does school attendance attenuate gender differences.	Female students carry a heavier workload and enjoy less leisure time than male students. But the difference in workloads is smaller compared to the one between adolescent girls and boys who do not attend school.

Table 2.A3. Select Methodologies of Time Use Data Collection

Method	Advantages	Disadvantages
Direct Observation		
In this method, the researcher observes what individuals do at particular times and records their activities.	▧ Does not require that the person observed is literate or have a western concept of time. ▧ Useful when activities are unstructured and fractioned in very small segments and where several activities are performed simultaneously	▧ Very researcher intensive. ▧ High costs ▧ Knowing that they are being observed, people tend to change their behavior ▧ Observer may have problems distinguishing market and non-market activities.
Stylized Questions		
This method is usually part of a questionnaire and consists of general questions on time spent on certain activities such as preparing meals on a given time period (day/week).	▧ Reliable in recording frequency of participation ▧ Less costly to process than diary data	▧ The total hours reported on various activities may exceed 24 hours. ▧ Dependent on perception and subjective calculation of time use. ▧ Time constrained stylized questions omit a large number of simultaneous activities ▧ Wording of stylized questions is hard and may lead to misinterpretations.
Stylized Activity List		
In this method, the questionnaire includes a list of daily activities and the person is asked how much time he/she spends on a given day doing each of these activities.	▧ Reliable in recording frequency of participation ▧ Less costly to process than diary data ▧ Depending on the design of the list, the accounting nature is maintained.	▧ The list provided may not include all possible daily activities. ▧ Wording of stylized questions is hard and may lead to misinterpretations.
Activity Log		
In this method, the person is asked to record on a questionnaire each time he/she engages in an activity and the time spent on this particular activity.		▧ Assumes that the person is literate and that they own a watch. ▧ Relies on the person's motivation and meticulousness in keeping the log.

(continued)

Table 2.A3. Select Methodologies of Time Use Data Collection (*Continued*)

Method	Advantages	Disadvantages
Stylized Time–Activity Matrix Similar to stylized activity list, this method includes a list of all possible activities. In this case time allocated should be 24 hours.		▨ Assumes that the person is able to remember all of his/her activities and can accurately assign them to the categories. ▨ Assumes good memory and good calculation skills.
Time Activity Matrix This method is an expanded version of the stylized time activity matrix. Includes an activity list and a list of time periods. The person recording the activities marks off the activities that he/she did in that time period. Each time period must have at least one activity.		
Interviewer Administered Time Diary In this method, the questionnaire does not provide a list of activities; the respondent describes each activity in his/her own words from the beginning to the end of a day.	▨ Provides consistency in time activity data by forcing full accounting of time. ▨ Depending on the design, may provide data on primary and simultaneous activities as well as sequential, spatial and social dimensions of the activity ▨ Minimizes recall bias	▨ Design may be too complicated especially in developing countries where the education level of interviewers and respondents tend to be low.
Tomorrow or Left Behind Diaries These are the same as time diaries but the diaries are left to respondents to fill out	▨ Since events can be recorded as they are performed, period covered can be more extensive than in other methods ▨ These are less expensive methods unless major review and corrections are needed	▨ Difficult to implement in illiterate societies. Diaries need to include pictures and extensive training of respondents may be required. ▨ Respondents may delay recording activities which may cause inaccuracies. ▨ Quality of diary may decline as respondents get less attentive. ▨ Problems in recording the sequence of activities may occur. Concurrent activities may not be recorded.

Source: Adapted from Budlender (2002) and Harvey and Taylor (2000).

CHAPTER 3

A Review of Empirical Evidence on Time Use in Africa from UN-Sponsored Surveys

Jacques Charmes[9]

This paper reviews some of the empirical evidence from time use surveys in Sub-Saharan Africa. Starting from a discussion of the 1993 revision of the System of National Accounts (SNA), the paper reviews definitions of work, both market-based and non-market work, paid and unpaid, and how these different types of work are classified and counted within and outside the SNA. The paper then summarizes the results of national time use surveys in four SSA countries, Benin, Madagascar, Mauritius, and South Africa, along with results from the time use module of the Ghana Living Standards Survey, paying particular attention to domestic work, the care economy, and non-economic activity. In conclusion, the paper examines some of the potential correlations between time use patterns and other development variables.

Time use surveys carried out at national level have for a long time been confined to industrialized countries where they were designed to measure the transformation toward a society and an economy of leisure. More recently, with the rise of unemployment rates, their results were used to show the changing roles of men and women in domestic activities. Yet, it is of course the measurement of domestic activities and of the care economy which always was their major objective.

This objective moved toward the transformation of these activities with the massive entry of women into the labor market and the rise of the elderly and the disabled in the population. In developing countries where time use surveys had been confined to village studies or very small and often non-representative samples, it is only recently that such nation-wide surveys have been implemented, with the support of UNDP programmes and the UN statistics division. India and Nepal (1999), Benin (1998), Nigeria (1999), South

---

9. The author is with the Institut de Recherche pour le Développement in Paris.

Africa (2000), Madagascar (2001), and more recently Mauritius (2003) have carried out such surveys. In the meantime however, some living standards surveys (especially in Ghana) included a time use section in their questionnaire in order to capture the main domestic or non-market activities.

In the context of developing countries, one of the major aims of time use surveys is to assess the underestimation of female participation in the labor force. In particular they aim at giving an estimate of women's contribution to the industrial sectors where they are often engaged in secondary activities which are not recorded by regular labor force surveys (especially in the processing of agricultural and food products, and also in textiles-clothing activities).

Moreover, results from time use surveys are of great help in the implementation of the 1993 SNA in countries where non-market production for own use consumption (including fetching water and wood) or capital formation is widely spread. But they are also used for the measurement of domestic activities in these countries as well. More recently, time use surveys have contributed to illustrate another dimension of poverty: lack of time due to multiple timetables (domestic work, care work, non-market economic activity) resulting in time poverty and low monetary income.

In this paper, we will first recall the definitions of work, market and non market, paid and unpaid, and economic activity as measured by the System of National Accounts (SNA) and its satellite accounts of household production in connection with the objectives of time use surveys. In the second section, the results of available time use surveys in various countries of Sub-Saharan Africa will be presented with particular reference to domestic work, care economy, non-market economic activity. Finally we will investigate the potential correlation between time use patterns and key development variables, especially in the perspective of future data collections and analyses.

Definitions of Work in the System of National Accounts

It is not here our purpose to come back into the details of the definitions of work and economic activity which we treated more extensively elsewhere (Charmes and Unni 2004; Charmes 2005). We would rather like to identify and specify some remaining topics of misunderstanding between feminist economists and national accountants in charge of the definition of what is to be counted in the Gross Domestic Product (GDP). We fully support the extensive notion of work and we recognize that it must be measured in the national accounts and the GDP. However, we think that for this purpose and for a better efficiency in the debates, it is crucial to use a terminology that is not confusing and misleading.

It is very usual to read in academic reports and articles that the exclusion of non-market work results in a downward bias in GDP calculations and other macroeconomic indicators. Or that current labor statistics do not capture the informal sector market work or the non-market work. Such assertions are incorrect.

Since 1993 (SNA 1993), production, as measured by the SNA, includes:

—the production of all goods and services destined for the market whether for sale or barter;
—the own-account production of all goods that are retained by their producers for their own final consumption or gross capital formation;

—the own-account production of housing services by owner-occupiers and personal services produced by households employing paid domestic staff; and

—the production of all goods and services provided free to individual households or collectively to the community by government units or non profit institutions serving households.

The SNA finds it useful to provide a tentative (but not complete) list of the types of production of goods for own consumption (SNA 1993, §6.24):

—"the production of agricultural products and their subsequent storage; the gathering of berries or other uncultivated crops; forestry; wood-cutting and the collection of firewood; hunting and fishing;

—the production of other primary products such as mining salt, cutting peat, the supply of water, etc.;

—the processing of agricultural products; the production of grain by threshing; the production of flour by milling; the curing of skins and the production of leather; the production and preservation of meat and fish products; the preservation of fruit by drying, bottling, etc.; the production of dairy products such as butter or cheese; the production of beer, wine, or spirits; the production of baskets and mats; etc.;

—other kinds of processing such as weaving cloth; dress making and tailoring; the production of footwear; the production of pottery, utensils and durables; making furniture or furnishings; etc."

As to the production of goods and services for own gross fixed capital formation, it includes the production of machine tools, dwellings and their extensions, and in rural areas such communal and collective construction activities as small dams, trails, irrigation channels, and so forth.

It is usually not very well known that such female time-consuming activities as firewood and water fetching fall within the boundaries of measured production. Ever since the SNA 1968, such activities are included, being considered as extractive activities and the National Accounts in various West African countries include them in their GDP calculations (for instance Burkina Faso; see Charmes 1989).

Referring now to labor force statistics, the resolution "concerning the economically active population, employment, unemployment and underemployment" (1982 International Conference of Labor Statisticians) unambiguously states that "the economically active population comprises all persons (…) who furnish the supply of labor for the production of economic goods and services as defined by the United Nations systems of national accounts."

The SNA distinguishes the "general production boundary" and the "production boundary in the SNA." In the general production boundary, production is defined as the physical process in which labor and assets are used to transform inputs of goods and services into outputs of other goods and services. Moreover, two conditions are required from goods and services to fall within the definition: "marketability" and adequacy with the "third-party" criterion. Marketability means that goods and services can (and not must) be sold in markets. The third-party criterion implies that the goods and services are "capable of being provided by one unit to another with or without charge," which excludes non-productive activities in an economic sense such as eating, sleeping, studying, and so forth, but includes the home and care economy (preparation of meals, care and training of children, care of the sick, handicapped, elderly, and so forth) as well as volunteer work. However, the definition of the production boundary in the SNA, for the purpose of measuring the GDP, restricts the scope by excluding the production of domestic and personal services by household members for consumption within the same household. Furthermore, the list of these domestic and personal services to be excluded (unless they are provided by paid employees) is enumerated (SNA, 1993, §6.20):

—the cleaning, decoration and maintenance of the dwelling occupied by the household, including small repairs of a kind usually carried out by tenants as well as owners,

—the cleaning, servicing and repair of household durables or other goods, including vehicles used for household purposes,

—the preparation and serving of meals,

—the care, training and instruction of children,

—the care of sick, infirm or old people, and

—the transportation of members of the households or their goods.

Besides household production, another issue that must be raised in the measurement of GDP and the definition of work and production is what constitutes "volunteer work." Here households are concerned as providers of work, but it is the non-profit institutions serving households (NPISH) which are the beneficiaries of this type of volunteer work. The value added contributing to the GDP must be attributed to the NPISH sector and not the household sector. Their output and value added are underestimated in the compilation of GDP because no monetary value is imputed to volunteer work while work is performed in the provision of services by these institutions. However, it is different whenever members of the household are performing such volunteer work for another household (and not for a collective institution), caring for the neighbor's children for instance.

Therefore, it is clear that SNA work and non-SNA work, market work and non-market work, paid work and unpaid work are not substitutable concepts. A part of non-market work is already included in the GDP (all production of goods for own consumption or capital formation, including collection of firewood and fetching water). This specific part cannot be referred to as "unpaid work" because it contributes to economic production and the former "unpaid family workers" are now called "contributing family workers" because their contribution to production has an equivalent on the income side. In particular, it cannot be said that "unpaid work" is not taken into account in the GDP if the contribution to the production of non-marketed goods (including fetching firewood or water) is part of "unpaid work." The following diagram tentatively explains how these various notions overlap.

The restrictive concept of "unpaid work" is limited to #4 in Figure 3.1: it exactly fits with the concept of "care economy," which is not part of the SNA as measured by the GDP. It is unambiguously outside the GDP. An extended concept of "unpaid work" includes box #3 also extended to all the self-employed engaged in the production of goods for own consumption. The widest concept of "unpaid work" would also extend it to those family workers who are engaged in economic units producing for the market (box #2). Categories 2

Figure 3.1.   To What Extent Do the Notions of Market/Non-Market Work, Paid/Unpaid Work and SNA/Non-SNA Work Overlap?

	Market work		Non-market work	
	Paid work	Unpaid work (contributing)	Unpaid work (contributing)	Unpaid work
SNA work	1	2 (family workers)	3 (family workers)	
Non-SNA work				4 (domestic and care work)

Notes: (1) Production of goods and services for the market by remunerated labor and remunerated self-employed. (2) Production of goods and services for the market by contributing family workers (belonging to economic units producing for the market. (3) Production of goods and services for own consumption or own capital formation of the household, by contributing family workers (belonging to economic units not producing for the market. (4) Production of domestic and care services in the extended SNA.

and 3 are already captured in the GDP even if we can agree that their capture is imperfect and that their contribution is underestimated.

These few remarks aim to clarify that women *per se* are not underestimated in the labor force or that their production is taken for nil in the GDP. There is of course a huge gap between the concepts as they are defined and their application in the statistical surveys: it is well known that labor force surveys are still undercounting women working in agriculture in some countries. Yet, progress has been made and the female activity rates in Sub-Saharan Africa, are among the highest in the world. Even if we admit that the number of women in the agricultural labor force is underestimated, this does not mean that their contribution to the agricultural production is underestimated. The reason for that is that in most countries, the output of agriculture is not based on the performance of individual farms but on estimates of areas and yields for the main crops. Consequently the contribution of women is really included even if it is not possible to determine their share.

Moreover the tentative measure of subsistence production as a separate aggregate often turns out to be imperfect because, for the time being, it is more and more difficult to find pure subsistence farms. Even the smallest farms that produce hardly enough for own-consumption of the household must sell at the harvest and buy when the storehouses are empty. In this sense, the fact that many women remain "contributing" family workers in their husband's farms does not mean that they are involved in subsistence production. As to the agricultural products they grow by themselves, it is well known that they usually trade them for cash. Therefore the distinction between commercial agriculture and subsistence agriculture has become more and more fuzzy and most labor force surveys and national accounts do not use it any more. Even when it is used, it does not mean that this "subsistence" agriculture is "non-market" agriculture.

However, there are still several reasons for the underestimation of women's contribution, due to the limits of the current concepts and methods of data collection.

A first reason is that women, more than men, are involved in multiple jobs. The measurement of pluri-activity is still a major challenge for survey statisticians. A better estimate of women's contribution to GDP is obtained in the countries where efforts have been made to measure their secondary activities (multiple jobs). Burkina Faso is a typical example of a country where the informal sector is principally urban, tertiary, and male as far as the main activities are taken into account, and becomes principally rural, manufacturing, and female, when multiple jobs are taken into account. Rural women are engaged in secondary activities, which mainly consist in the processing of agricultural products and food products.

A second reason results from the first one: statistical surveys generally fail to measure these female manufacturing activities that are hidden behind agricultural, primary, or trade activities. The bulk of the female labor force, especially in the informal sector, is in agriculture and in trade. Trade is very often the last stage of diversified female activities starting with growing agricultural products or collecting natural products, processing them (food products, mats and baskets, textiles, and so forth) and finally selling them. Where only this last stage (trade) is captured, or the first one (agriculture or gathering), then the value added of female activities is often underestimated. Moreover where these processing activities lead into domestic activities (for example, winnowing and crushing cereals for the preparation of meals), they often remain unmeasured.

Possible directions for future progress in the measurement and understanding of female pluri-activity lie in time use surveys, but it may require, for instance, a sufficient decomposition of the activities involved in the preparation of meals.

Measurement of Work in Time Use Surveys in Sub-Saharan Africa

Four time use surveys have been conducted at national level in Sub-Saharan Africa since 1998 (the 1998 time use survey in Nigeria was a pilot survey implemented in four states and Lagos at 243 households, and the results were not published). The South African survey was a specific *ad hoc* survey, while the Benin and Madagascar surveys were specific surveys attached to continuous permanent surveys, and the Mauritius survey was a specific module included in the multi-purpose household questionnaire.

Furthermore, the Ghana Living Standards Survey (GLSS) has included questions on time use for housekeeping activities in its third round (1991–92), fourth round (1998–99) and fifth round (2003–04). However in this case, it is not a full-range questionnaire and the comparability with the other four countries is debatable.[10] Before presenting the major results of these recent time use surveys, it is necessary to recall that, when analyzing time use data, one must remember that there are two types of results and indicators. A first type refers to averages covering the total population that has been surveyed (without regarding whether or not this population was involved in any of the recorded activities; the total number of hours is divided by the total population). A second type refers to averages covering only the population involved in performing the activities. Moreover, the averages (presented on a daily or weekly basis) are calculated on a complete year of 365 days:

---

10. At the World Bank workshop at which this paper was presented in November 2005, other case studies were presented and are included in Part II and III of this volume.

the respondents have been interviewed at random for any day in the week and any week in the year, so that a part of the surveyed population was interviewed during weekends, holidays, non-working days, days of sickness or days of social events. This is why the figures presented in the tables may be viewed as lower than expected. For example, a wage-earner in the formal sector is expected to work at least 8 hours a day, but in a complete year, she or he may have worked only 6 or 7 hours a day.

Table 3.1 compares the various characteristics of the time use surveys for the five countries, in terms of sample size, age of the respondents, and methods of data collection. Despite their differences, it can be considered that the results for the four time use surveys are comparable; only the Ghanaian case is to be looked at separately. It must also be noted that in Benin and Madagascar, the surveys were carried out in the agricultural off-season. However, the results seem coherent with the results of other surveys. Table 3.2 provides the global results of the surveys in the four countries with time use surveys.

Time devoted to production activities as measured by the SNA (and including activities such as fetching water or collecting firewood) varies from a little bit less than 2 hours (in South Africa and Mauritius) to nearly 3 hours in Madagascar and 4 hours in Benin. It has to be borne in mind that such statistics include active and inactive persons, the youth as well as the elderly.

The ratio of females to males is the smallest in Mauritius where women spend only 39 percent of what men spend in SNA production activities and it is the highest in Benin where women and men spend the same amount of time. In South Africa and Madagascar, the ratio is around 60 percent.

Regarding work at large, women spend more time than men at work. Duration ranges from 5 hours and 43 minutes in South Africa to 7 hours and 23 minutes in Benin (and 6 hours and a half in Mauritius and 6 hours and 36 minutes in Madagascar), so that they exceed men by nearly a half in Benin (47 percent), 29 percent in South Africa, 18 percent in Madagascar and 6 percent in Mauritius. This is because their involvement in domestic and care activities is much bigger than men's: 4.7 times more in Madagascar, nearly 4 times (3.79) in Mauritius, 3.04 times more in South Africa and 3.1 more in Benin. In Benin, Madagascar and South Africa, time spent in domestic and care activities is relatively comparable: 3 hours and 28 to 48 minutes (against 4 hours and a half in Mauritius), compared to a little bit less or more than one hour for men in the four countries.

Finally, the share of SNA activities in work at large ranges from 29.5 percent (Mauritius) to 33.5 percent (South Africa), 44.2 percent (Madagascar) and 53.0 percent (Benin) for women, compared with 71.7 percent in South Africa, 77.8 percent in Benin, 80.2 percent in Mauritius and 86.1 percent in Madagascar for men. In other words, domestic, care, and volunteer activities account for more than 50 percent and up to more than two thirds of work in its broad sense.

It is interesting to note that in Ghana, when adding up the housekeeping activities mentioned in the questionnaire (childcare, sweeping, cooking, garbage disposal), the time spent by women is 5 hours 42 minutes (compared with 3 hours 8 minutes for men). The ratio of females to males for domestic and care activities is then comparable to Benin (1.81 compared with 1.75), but at a much higher level, meaning that the method of data collection tends to overestimate the time spent in these activities. Or, more likely, it tends to capture some of these activities as simultaneous activities (especially childcare).

Table 3.1. Characteristics of the Time Use Surveys in Five Sub-Saharan African Countries

	Benin (1998)	South Africa (2000)	Madagascar (2001)	Mauritius (2003)	Ghana (1991–92 and 1998–99)
Type of survey	Specific attached to a permanent survey (same sample)	Specific ad hoc survey	Specific attached to a permanent survey (parallel sample)	Time use diary module in a continuous multipurpose household survey	Short and incomplete time use module in a continuous living standard survey
Sample size (households)	3,206	8,564	2,663	6,480	5,998
Sample size (individuals)	12,604	14,553	7,743	19,907	25,664
Age	6–65	10+	6–65	10+	7+
Time slots	15mn	30mn	15mn	30mn	No
Method of data collection	Pre-listed Diary 24 hours past day	Diary 24 hours past day	Pre-listed Diary 24 hours past day	Diary 24 hours past day	Average time spent in selected housekeeping activities in the last 7 days
Simultaneous activities	Yes	Yes	Yes	Yes	No
Seasonality activities	No (March–April)	Yes	No (October—November)	Yes (540 households per month)	Yes
Classification of activities	Pre-listing of 63 activities classified SNA/non SNA	UN classification	Pre-listing of 77 activities classified SNA/non SNA	UN classification	Ad hoc classification

Table 3.2. Time Devoted per Day to Economic Activity and to Work, by Gender in Various Countries (In hours and minutes)

	Benin (1998)			South Africa (2000)			Madagascar (2001)			Mauritius (2003)		
	Women	Men	Women/Men	Women	Men	Women/Men	Women	Men	Women/Men	Women	Men	Women/Men
SNA production	3h 55mn	3h 55mn	100%	1h 55mn	3h 10mn	61%	2h 55mn	4h 50mn	60%	1h 56mn	4h 56mn	39%
Non SNA production: Domestic activities	3h 28mn	1h 7mn	310%	3h 48mn	1h 15mn	304%	3h 41mn	47mn	470%	4h 37mn	1h 13mn	379%
Work	7h 23mn	5h 2mn	147%	5h 43mn	4h 25mn	129%	6h 36mn	5h 37mn	118%	6h 33mn	6h 9mn	106%
% SNA in work	53.0%	77.8%	68.2%	33.5%	71.7%	47.0%	44.2%	86.1%	51.0%	29.5%	80.2%	36.8%

Source: Table elaborated on basis of the results of national time use surveys: INSAE/PNUD (1998), Enquête emploi du temps au Bénin, Méthodologie et résultats, Cotonou; Statistics South Africa (2001), How South African Women and Men spend their time, A survey of time use, Pretoria; INSTAT- DSM/PNUD-MAG/97/007: EPM 2001- Module Emploi du Temps, Antananarivo; Republic of Mauritius, Central Statistics Office (2004), Continuous Multi-Purpose Household Survey 2003, Main results of the time use study.

Table 3.3. Classifications of SNA Non-Market Activities Used in South Africa, Benin and Madagascar

SNA Non-Market Activities	
South Africa	**Benin, Madagascar**
Crop farming	Agriculture,
	Gardening
Tending animals, fish farming	Animal husbandry
	Small cattle
	Cattle
	Poultry
Hunting, gathering	Hunting
	Fishing
	Gathering
	Forestry
Digging, stone cutting and carving	
	Crushing
Food processing and preservation	Processing agricultural products for food
	Drying food products
	Other processing for self-consumption
Preparing/selling food & beverages	
Making/selling textiles/craft	Spinning
	Weaving
	Embroidering
	Basket making
	Mat making
Building and extension of dwelling	

If we now detail the SNA non-market activities in the various countries, it is necessary to look at the different classifications used. Table 3.3 compares the two classifications for South Africa (which follows the UN classification) and for Benin and Madagascar (where some 70 activities were pre-listed on the questionnaire). Although there is not an exact correspondence in the wording of activities, (there is one more activity for South Africa: digging and stone cutting and carving) and the list is more detailed for the two other countries, it can be assumed that all the spectrum of SNA non-market activities is well covered.

Table 3.4 is based on the shorter classification (South Africa) and the data for Benin and Madagascar have been adapted and aggregated accordingly. Fetching water and collecting firewood are classified in SNA non-market activities although South Africa put them in non-SNA productive activities (see preceding section). Specific tables are prepared for those two activities (Tables 3.5, 3.6, and 3.7). Moreover, South Africa does not distinguish SNA market from SNA non-market, while Benin and Madagascar have recorded the

Table 3.4. Time Spent per Day on SNA Non-Market Activities in Three Countries (In hours and minutes)

	Benin (1998)		South Africa (2000)		Madagascar (2001)	
	Women	Men	Women	Men	Women	Men
Crop farming	11	29	5	4	20	29
Tending animals, fish farming		13	1	10	9	37
Hunting, gathering	4	11		1	5	5
Digging, stone cutting and carving				1		
Fetching water	45	12	8	3	27	9
Collecting firewood	16	4	6	3	7	13
Food processing and preservation	26	8			20	3
Preparing/selling food & beverages			2	1		
Making/selling textiles/craft	2	2	3	1	16	
Building and extension of dwelling			1	3	6	1
Total	1h 44	1h 19	24	27	1h 50	1h 37

Note: For South Africa, the results are based on the final table providing time spent by the persons engaged in each detailed activity. Consequently total time spent by persons engaged was divided by the total sample.

National figures are based on a distribution of the population between urban and rural areas as follows: 30/70% for Madagascar, 36/64% for Benin.

Source: Calculations are based on the same sources as Table 3.2.

non-market activities which were not declared as main economic activities. Notwithstanding these differences, the gap is huge in favor of Benin and Madagascar (meaning for instance that farming for own-account is nearly negligible in South Africa).

Tables 3.4 and 3.5 highlight huge differences between Benin and Madagascar on the one hand and South Africa on the other hand.

Table 3.5. Time Spent per Day in SNA Non-Market Activities in Three Countries as a Share of Total SNA Production (In hours and minutes)

	Benin (1998)			South Africa (2000)			Madagascar (2001)		
	Women	Men	Women /Men	Women	Men	Women /Men	Women	Men	Women /Men
SNA production	3h 55mn	3h 55mn	100.0	1h 55mn	3h 10mn	60.5	2h 55mn	4h 50mn	60.5
SNA non-market	1h 44mn	1h 19mn	131.6	24mn	27mn	88.8	1h 50mn	1h 37mn	113.4
Non-market in %	44.3	33.6		20.9	14.2		62.9	33.4	

Source: See sources for Table 3.2.

Table 3.6. Time Spent by Women in Food Crops Work and by Men in Food Crop and Export Crops, Center-South Cameroon, 1976

	January	February	March	April	May	June	July	August	September	October	November	December	Average
Women													
Number of observations	38	42	64	85	71	72	69	45	38	38	33	33	52.3
Number of days per month	15	14	18	19	18	19	19	13	17	15	13	16	16.3
Number of hours per day	5	4.8	5.5	6.2	5.9	5.6	5.9	5.8	6.3	5.7	6.0	6.4	5.8
Men													
Number of observations	39	54	66	68	68	65	62	56	41	38	25	20	50.2
Number of days per month	11	13	15	15	17	16	16	14	17	16	17	16	15.3
Number of hours per day	4.7	4.7	4.6	4.3	4.7	4.2	4.7	4.6	4.2	4.4	4.6	4.6	4.5
Women/Men (hours)	106.4%	102.1%	119.6%	144.2%	125.5%	133.3%	125.5%	126.1%	150.0%	129.5%	130.4%	139.1%	127.3%

Source: Leplaideur (1978).

Are these differences due to differences in the level of development? Probably not. All the more so as the UN classification of time use activities used in the South African survey does not distinguish non-market activities and only distinguishes between work for establishments and activities not for establishments. For example, "preparing/selling food and beverages" or "making/selling textiles and craft" are activities to be classified in "market production" if at least a part of the production is sold on the market and in "non-market production" if there is no sale at all. We have already stressed that the distinction market/non-market was more and more misleading because there is no way to identify this distinction in the usual permanent statistical survey. However, in the Benin and Madagascar time use surveys, these activities have been recorded after the main and secondary activities had been declared by the respondents: this means that in the absence of time use survey, these activities would not have been recorded. Yet, the time devoted to them is high.

The SNA non-market activities account for 44.3 percent in women's time contribution to SNA production in Benin, and for 62.9 percent in Madagascar (against 20.9 percent in South Africa). In these two countries, men's time contribution to SNA production through the SNA non-market activities is about one third. The gap between women and men is mainly due to the activities of fetching water and collecting firewood.

The sexual division of labor in SNA non-market activities clearly stands out from Table 3.4: crop farming and especially animal husbandry are male activities, while processing of food and agricultural products is a female activity. Craft activities are male or female activities depending on national circumstances and also the seasons. Making mats and baskets is an important female activity in Madagascar as shown in Table 3.4.

This type of results does not say much about the sexual division of labor in agriculture (except the one mentioned between crop farming and animal husbandry). It must be noted here that time use surveys are not tailored and designed to record the details of farming work. For instance, time use surveys do not record explicitly what type of work was performed by the respondent in his (her) main economic activity: did the furniture-maker cut wood, or assemble the furniture, or paint the furniture? Did the farmer sow, plough, hoe, or harvest? The time use surveys do not intend to split up the production process into its various stages.

In this sense the recent time use surveys diverge from the former village studies designed to measure the diversity of farming works and the sexual division of labor in agriculture. Yet changes occurring in this field obviously have an impact on time use in general: for instance, when hoeing was mechanized in rice fields in Madagascar in the early 1970s, this type of female work became male work.

However, previous surveys conducted in the 1970s and focusing on time use in agricultural activities, provide a different picture: they show that women were spending more time than men in agricultural production, even though they were excluded from export crop production. The study carried out in 1976 by Leplaideur (1978) among a hundred male and female farmers in the center-south of Cameroon over an entire year, illustrates for example a huge gender gap in the opposite direction within SNA work itself. It shows that women spent on average more than 16 days per month and 5.8 hours per day in food crop activities while men spent 15 days per month and 4.5 hours per day in food crops and export crops. In total, the ratio of women to men in agricultural work rises up to 127.3 percent with peaks around 150 percent in April and September (Table 3.6).

It must be noted however that such results are not strictly comparable with the results of the time use surveys analyzed in this paper. In this case, the hundred persons interviewed are adults entirely dedicated to these activities during the period, while in the time use surveys the results are based on the total population (adults, youth, elderly, active or inactive, dedicated and not dedicated, captured during working days and not working days). Also these results show how useful it would be that time use surveys adequately and precisely capture the various operations included in SNA economic activities.

Fetching water and collecting firewood deserve some more attention not only because gender differentiation is high in these activities, but also because they often continue to be classified with non-SNA productive activities. However, "fetching water" accounted for 1 percent of the GDP in the 1974 National Accounts of Burkina Faso (Charmes 1989), an estimation based on household consumption and not on time use. It has also given rise to some methodological research. Whittington, Winming, and Roche (1990) propose an appropriate value of time spent on this activity. Findings of the research conducted in Ukunda, Kenya, suggest a value approximately equivalent to the wage rate for unskilled labor, making attractive and profitable a technology based on piped distribution which would also be an opportunity for saving and sparing women's time.

Table 3.7 summarizes the results for four countries, while Tables 3.8 and 3.9 provide the information for the respondents engaged in the activity (and not an average for the whole population) and for a specific age-group.

The definition of "fetching water" is unambiguous in principle. In fact the collection of water can also be performed as a task of a production process for the main economic activity. However, in time use surveys this activity is clearly associated with an activity *per se*, to be included either in SNA production (which is correct) or in the domestic production.

It is slightly different for "collecting firewood." Some surveys or classifications have opted for a wider denomination such as "collecting fuel." They also distinguish a category "chopping wood" and more exactly "chopping wood, lighting fire and heating water not for immediate cooking purposes," a wording that might be misleading because women can go collecting and chopping wood, not for immediate cooking purposes. In South Africa, this second activity involves many more persons but requires much less time than the activity "collecting fuel." The two activities have been added up for South Africa in the following tables. However, the impact is limited. Again, "collecting firewood" and "cutting wood" are intermediate activities of the production process for charcoal or salt extraction. As was shown for Guinea (Geslin 1997), these two activities take 1 hour and 10 minutes of women engaged in salt extraction (on a working day of more than 13 hours and a half) and nearly one hour for men (in a working day of 16 hours).

It is in rural Benin that "fetching water" takes the more time for women (more than one hour per day on average according to Table 3.7). Women involved in this activity (72 percent of women of all age-groups; Table 3.8) spend more than 1 hour and a half (1h 38 minutes). At national level (urban and rural) the "fetching water" daily chore takes 45 minutes for women, and the burden of "collecting firewood" takes 7 to 8 times more time in the countryside than in the cities.

"Collecting firewood" generally takes less time (from 23 minutes in rural Benin to 37 minutes in rural Ghana for women) and this burden is more often shared by men: in rural Madagascar, men spend 27 minutes a day to this task against 8 minutes for women.

Table 3.7. Time Spent on Fetching Water and Collecting Firewood by Women and Men (In hours and minutes)

		Benin (1998)			South Africa (2000)			Madagascar (2001)			Ghana (1998–99)		
		Women	Men	Women/Men	Women	Men	Women/Men	Women	Men	Women/Men	Women	Men	Women/Men
Fetching water	Urban	16	6	267%				16	10	160%	33	31	106%
	Rural	1h 2	16	388%				32	8	400%	44	34	129%
	Urban and rural	45	12	375%	8	3	267%	27	9	300%	41	33	124%
Collecting firewood	Urban	3	1	300%				3	6	50%	44	51	86%
	Rural	23	5	460%				8	27	30%	37	28	132%
	Urban and rural	16	4	400%	6	3	200%	7	13	54%	37	30	123%

Source: See sources for Table 3.2; Ghana Statistical Service (2000), Ghana Living Standards Survey, Report of the 4th Round (GLSS 4), Accra.

Table 3.8. Time Spent on Fetching Water and Collecting Firewood by Women and Men Engaged in the Activity (In hours and minutes)

		Benin (1998)			South Africa (2000)			Madagascar (2001)		
		Women	Men	Women/Men	Women	Men	Women/Men	Women	Men	Women/Men
Fetching water	Urban	47	40	118%				56	54	104%
	Rural	1h 38	1h 15	131%				62	56	111%
	Urban and rural	1h 2	1h 2	100%	1h 2	46	135%	1h 2	55	113%
Collecting firewood	Urban	1h 5	1h 11	92%				1h 6	1h 13	90%
	Rural	1h 50	1h 30	122%				1h 14	1h 31	81%
	Urban and rural	1h 14	1h 23	89%	2h 17	2h 14	102%	1h 12	1h 26	84%

Source: See sources for Table 3.2.

Table 3.9. Time Spent per Day on Fetching Water and Collecting Firewood by Girls and Boys Aged 6 to 14 (Benin and Madagascar) or 7 to 14 (Ghana) (In hours and minutes)

		Benin (1998)			Madagascar (2001)			Ghana (1998–99)		
		Women	Men	Women/ Men	Women	Men	Women/ Men	Women	Men	Women/ Men
Fetching water	Urban	16	10	160%	17	17	100%			
	Rural	1h3	24	263%	37	16	231%			
	Urban and rural	46	19	242%	31	16	194%	41	38	108%
Collecting firewood	Urban	2	2	100%	2	6	33%			
	Rural	17	7	243%	7	24	29%			
	Urban and rural	12	5	240%	6	19	32%	30	29	103%

Source: See sources for Table 3.6.

In urban Ghana as well, men spend 51 minutes daily to collect firewood (against 44 minutes for women).

Such statistics multiplied by the number of days in a year and the total population lead to a macroeconomic figure of the total number of hours spent in water fetching or collecting firewood at national level. These figures can be valued to provide an estimate of production, which is equivalent to the value added, provided there is no intermediate consumption.

The estimate amounts to 2 million hours for men and 4 million hours for women in Ghana in 1992, which makes 6 million hours in total for water fetching. The total figure is 3.1 million hours for collecting firewood (2.2 million for women and 0.8 million hours for men; GSS 1995).

Table 3.8 shows that for those persons in charge of the burden, "fetching water" or "collecting firewood" takes between one hour and more than two hours a day (in South Africa). "Fetching water" and "collecting firewood" are typically associated with child labor. In Benin, Madagascar and also in Ghana, girls and boys spend more time fetching water than the adults (Table 3.9). Furthermore, in Benin and Madagascar where the child population has been classified between those who go to school and those who don't, it seems that attending school does not prevent children from being charged with this task. The only significant difference is for rural girls in Benin who spent 50 minutes per day fetching water (compared to 63 minutes for all girls aged 6–14). On the contrary, "collecting firewood" is less time-consuming for boys and girls than for adults. Still, the number of minutes spent per day on this task is not very far from the population average.

The GLSS gives an opportunity for analyzing a short trend (from 1991 to 1999 and soon to 2004) for these two activities. Table 3.10 synthesizes the observations in terms of the number of persons involved and the time spent (in average for the total population, involved or not) in water fetching and wood fetching. For both activities, the number of persons involved has decreased by 8 percentage points for women as well as for men.

Table 3.10. Trends in Number of Persons Involved and Time Spent per Day in Water and Wood Fetching in Ghana, 1991–92 and 1998–99

		Number of persons involved (%)		Number of minutes per day and per person	
		1991–92	1998–99	1991–92	1998–99
Water fetching	Women	68	60.2	40	41
	Men	45	37.7	21	33
	Both	57	49.1	31	38
Wood fetching	Women	43	34.6	22	37
	Men	24	16.0	9	30
	Both	34	25.6	16	35

Source: Based on Ghana Statistical Service (1995), Ghana Living Standards Survey, Report of the 3rd Round (GLSS 3), September 1991–September 1992, Accra, and Ghana Statistical Service (2000), Ghana Living Standards Survey, Report of the 4th Round (GLSS 4), Accra.

At the same time, the number of minutes spent in performing the activities has been increasing for water fetching (12 minutes for men, but only 1 minute for women) as well as for wood fetching (15 minutes for women, and 21 minutes for men). Although it is difficult to interpret these results in the absence of qualitative data and surveys, it seems obvious that they are correlated to a better access to sources of drinking water and less need to resort on wood for cooking. Yet, for those households that did not benefit from the improvements in infrastructure or equipment (such as tap water or improved stoves for instance), they had to go further to satisfy their needs, because of deforestation.

Looking now at non-SNA productive activities, we again compare the various classifications used (Table 3.11). The South African and Mauritius classifications (UN classification) are much more detailed than the pre-listed classification used in Benin and Madagascar, not to mention Ghana, which used only four categories.

A major difference is that the various caring activities in the South African survey distinguish between "spontaneous" caring and "prompted" caring. For instance supervising children allows for performing another activity while taking care of them is a complete activity that cannot allow performing another one. The fact that the other classifications do not make such a distinction means that both forms of activities are recorded in the survey. Furthermore, where (as in Ghana) there is only a short list of activities, there is a risk of overestimation of the time spent in these activities, particularly for men.

The two classifications identify domestic and care work on the one hand, and volunteer work on the other hand. Here the two classifications are definitely not comparable and the Ghana survey does not even record such activities. The South African survey and classification are much better and complete and should be used. It must be noted however that, in National Accounts, the value added by these activities must be split into household production (care of non-household members) and production of the Non-Profit Institutions serving Households (NPISH).

Regarding the core domestic activities which are preparing meals and washing up, washing-ironing, and care of children, the gap between women and men is huge: women's contribution varies from 13 or 12 times men's (for preparing meals) and 10 or 9 times (for both meals and wash up) in Madagascar, Benin and Mauritius, to 2 or 4 times in Ghana and South Africa respectively.

The gap is even more accentuated for "washing-ironing": it varies from 38 to 23 times in Mauritius and Madagascar to 3 to 4 times in Benin and South Africa.

As for childcare, it takes 13 times more time of women than of men in South Africa, 7 times in Benin, 6 in Madagascar, 3 in Mauritius, and nearly 2 times in Ghana.

The duration for the preparation of meals and the wash up are very comparable in the five countries, notwithstanding the variations in the methodology. It takes generally between one and a half and two hours per day per woman (this average including those women who are not engaged in the activity). The methodology makes a difference for men: in Ghana where the survey did not use the diary, the design of the question results in a rather high figure for men (55 minutes) which may be exaggerated.

The same remark applies for "washing-ironing": the duration is approximately the same in all countries (more or less half an hour per day).

"Care of children" takes from half an hour to three quarters of an hour for women against 4 to 13 minutes for men. A huge difference is observed in Ghana where time devoted to care of children takes 3 hours and 24 minutes a day for women, an 1 hour and

Table 3.11. Classifications of Non-SNA Activities Used in South Africa, Benin, Madagascar, and Ghana

Non-SNA Activities (Domestic, care)		
South Africa	Benin, Madagascar	Ghana
Preparing food and drinks	Preparing meals	Cooking
	Washing up	
Cleaning and upkeep of dwelling		Sweeping
Care of textiles	Washing, Ironing	
Shopping	Shopping	
Accessing government services	Accessing government services	
Household management		
Home improvements		
Pet care		
Household maintenance	Household maintenance	Garbage disposal
	Other Maintenance	
Fitting, Maintaining tools and machinery	Repairing house or apparels	
Physical care of children (spontaneous)	Caring for children	Childcare
Physical care of children (prompted)		
Teaching of household children (spontaneous)	Teaching of household children	
Teaching of household children (prompted)		
Accompanying children (spontaneous)	Accompanying children	
Accompanying children (prompted)		
Physical care of non-child household members	Caring for adults, handicapped, elderly	
Accompanying adults		
Supervising those needing care (spontaneous)		
Supervising those needing care (prompted)		
Care of household members n.e.c		
Non-SNA Activities (volunteer)		
Community organised construction		
Community organised work	Preparing food for ceremonies	
	Other Manufacturing for ceremonies	

(continued)

Table 3.11 Classifications of Non-SNA Activities Used in South Africa, Benin, Madagascar, and Ghana (*Continued*)

Non-SNA Activities (Domestic, care)		
South Africa	Benin, Madagascar	Ghana
Organizational volunteering		
Participation in meetings	Participation in meetings (associations)	
	Participation in meetings (religious)	
Involvement in civic responsibilities		
Caring for non-household children (spontaneous)		
Caring for non-household children (prompted)		
Caring for non-household adults (spontaneous)		
Caring for non-household adults (prompted)		
Other informal help to other households		
Community services n.e.c		

Note: The detailed classification for Mauritius is not given because only the main results of the survey have been published.

47 minutes a day for men. One may wonder whether the methodology used for data collection can be responsible for such a difference with the other surveys. The capture of simultaneous activities may be an explanation. In Benin and Madagascar, rural women involved in the activity spend more than two hours caring for children. Another issue that can be raised in this respect is the difficulty to record "caring for children" when this activity is embedded within the main economic activity. In such a case, the methodological efforts for capturing simultaneous activities might be insufficient because the capture of simultaneous activities is focussing on the activities which are performed at home or in the household, rather than on the work site, especially if the individual works for an establishment. Here again, it is interesting to note that Geslin (1997), recording the working hours of Guinean women extracting salt, included more than 1 hour for childcare in a working day of 13 and a half hours. Even if such a figure seems low, the point here is that simultaneity of tasks or activities may be missed when they occur during the usual SNA market activities.

From a methodological point of view, it seems clear that the more detailed and contextualized the activities in caring children (physical care, teaching, accompanying; spontaneous, prompted), the longer the time spent and recorded for these activities. The same remark should be valid for "caring for adults." However, even in South Africa, time spent on "caring for adults" is remarkably low for women and men: 6 minutes for women against 2 minutes for men in South Africa, and only 2 minutes against 1 minute in the other countries.

Table 3.12. Time Spent on Non-SNA Productive Activities in Five African Countries (in hours and minutes)

	Benin 1998			Ghana (1998–99)			South Africa (2000)			Madagascar (2001)			Mauritius (2003)		
	Women	Men	Women/Men	Women	Men	Women/Men	Women	Men	Women/Men	Women	Men	Women/Men	Women	Men	Women/Men
Preparing meals	1h 15	6	1250%	1h 47	55	195%	1h 24	19	443%	1h 34	7	1343%	1h 56	12	967%
Washing up	17	4	425%							22	4	550%			
Washing, Ironing	22	7	314%				26	6	403%	23	1	2300%	38	1	3800%
Shopping	22	20	110%				7	6	116%	18	7	257%	15	20	75%
Accessing government services	1	2	50%				1	1			1				
Household maintenance	28	10	280%	20	14	143%	48	24	200%	23	4	575%	1	7	14%
Other Maintenance	7	6	117%				26	6	403%	3	6	50%			
Repairing house or apparels	1	6	17%				2	2		1	8	13%			
Caring for children							24	2	1580%	32	5	640%	39	11	355%
Teaching of household children	29	4	725%	3h 24	1h 48	189%	2	0	419%	1			3	2	150%
Accompanying children	2	0					1			2	1	200%			
Caring for adults, handicapped, elderly							6	2	390%	2	1	200%	2	1	200%
Help to other households							2	3	55%				3	3	100%
Community services	4	2	200%				2	4	62%	2			1	1	100%
Total	3h 28	1h 7	310%	5h 31	2h 57	187%	3h 48	1h 15	305%	3h 41	47	470%	4h 36	1h 13	378%

Source: See sources in Table 3.6.

When looking at the persons engaged in the task of "supervising those needing care," it takes more than one hour, plus another hour for "accompanying" with a number of women which is five times the number of men. Even if there seems to be a kind of specialization between household members caring for the adults who need it, time required for these tasks remains limited.

However, the fact that this space of time is three times longer in South Africa compared with the other countries could be related to the burden of caring for the sick and especially those members of the household who are infected by HIV/AIDS.

Household maintenance is also a female activity, which is somewhat counterbalanced by other maintenance and repairing house, tools or apparels among men.

Lastly "shopping" is shared rather equally between women and men, except in Madagascar, while "accessing to government services" is more a male task.

Finally, "volunteer activities" seem to be insufficiently harmonised and data collection insufficiently systematized to be validly compared among countries. For South Africa and Mauritius where such harmonization and systematization exist, women and men spend on average 2 to 3 minutes a day helping other households on a rather equal sharing basis. Help of the community takes from 1 minute a day for men and women in Mauritius to 4 minutes for women in Benin and for men in South Africa.

In total, women spend more time than men in non-SNA productive activities: more than 4 times in Madagascar, more than 3 times in Benin, South Africa and Mauritius, and nearly twice in Ghana. Time length is the higher in Ghana with 5 hours and 31 minutes for women against 2 hours and 57 minutes for men (but that could be due to methodological reasons), and in Mauritius (4 hours 36 minutes for women against 1 hour and 13 minutes for men). It is lower in Benin, Madagascar and South Africa with respectively 3 hours and 28 minutes, 3 hours and 41 minutes, 3 hours and 48 minutes (against 1 hour and 7 minutes, 47 minutes and 1 hour and 15 minutes for men).

Finally, Table 3.13 provides the distribution of time between SNA work, Work outside SNA and non-work activities during an average day in four sub-Saharan countries. Within a 24 hours-day, women devote from 8 to 16 percent of their time to SNA work (against 13 to 20 percent for men) and from 13 to 18 percent to domestic and care work (against 4 to 6 percent for men), which makes from 23 to 30 percent for work (against 20 to 26 percent for men). Physiological needs and personal care take from 49 to 55 percent of women's daytime and from 48 to 54 percent for men.

It is interesting to compare these data with the results of surveys conducted in 1984 among two populations in southwest Cameroon (Tables 3.14 and 3.15). These surveys are very specific because they were looking at activity patterns and energy consumption. To this end, they measured time spent in the various activities with stopwatches on small samples of individuals. Although the results are not strictly comparable with those of the time use surveys examined in this paper (regarding the scope and coverage of the surveys, the date and the type of populations surveyed), it is interesting to note (Tables 3.16 and 3.17) that time devoted to physiological needs and personal care is higher in these specific surveys (from 53 to 55 percent for women, against 55 to 59 percent for men). The levels of domestic and care work are much higher for women (from 29 to 34 percent) and lower for men (from 3 to 5 percent) so that the gender gap is broader. The same observations but in the reverse sense can be made for SNA work: it is lower for women (from 6 to 10 percent)

Table 3.13. Comparisons of Daily Time Use for Women and Men in Four Sub-Saharan African Countries

Activities	South Africa 2000			Bénin 1998			Madagascar 2001			Mauritius (2003)		
	Women	Men	Both sexes	Women	Men	Both sexes	Women	Men	Both sexes	Women	Men	Both sexes
SNA activities	1h 55mn	3h 10mn	2h 30mn	3h 55mn	3h 55mn	3h 55mn	2h 55mn	4h 50mn	3h 50mn	1h 56mn	4h 56mn	3h 25mn
Of which:												
– non-market				35mn	15mn	25mn	50mn	55mn	50mn			
– fetching water	10mn	5mn	5mn	15mn	5mn	10mn	15mn	10mn	15mn			
– collecting firewood				5mn	0	0	5mn	5mn	5mn			
Domestic and care activities	3h 35mn	1h 25mn	2h 35mn	3h 15mn	1h	2h 10mn	3h 45mn	55mn	2h 25mn	4h 37mn	1h 13mn	2h 56mn
Work	5h 30mn	4h 35mn	5h 5mn	7h 10mn	4h 55mn	6h 5mn	6h 40mn	5h 45mn	6h 15mn	6h 33mn	6h 9mn	6h 21mn
School, studying	1h 35 mn	1h 50mn	1h 40mn	1h 5mn	1h 50mn	1h 30mn	1h 35mn	1h 55mn	1h 45mn	1h 5mn	1h 7mn	1h 6mn
Social activities	2h 10mn	2h 20mn	2h 15mn	1h 25mn	1h 55mn	1h 45mn	35mn	40mn	35mn	1h 45mn	2h 28mn	2h 6mn
Leisure	2h 5mn	2h 35mn	2h 20mn	55mn	1h 40mn	1h 15mn	2h 15mn	2h 40mn	2h 25mn	1h 48mn	1h 41mn	1h 45mn
Commuting	1h	1h 25mn	1h 15mn	30mn	50mn	45mn	40mn	1h	50mn			
Sleeping, eating, resting, personal care	12h 15mn	12h 5mn	12h 10mn	12h 50mn	12h 50mn	12h 50mn	13h 10mn	13h 5mn	13h 5mn	11h 49mn	11h 35mn	11h 42mn

Source: Table elaborated on basis of the results of national time use surveys : INSAE/PNUD (1998), Enquête emploi du temps au Bénin, Méthodologie et résultats, Cotonou; Statistics South Africa (2001), How South African Women and Men spend their time, A survey of time use, Pretoria; INSTAT- DSM/PNUD-MAG/97/007: EPM 2001- Module Emploi du Temps, Antananarivo; Republic of Mauritius, Central Statistics Office (2004), Continuous Multi-Purpose Household Survey 2003, Main results of the time use study.

Table 3.14. Time Use among the Yassa of Campo (Southwest Cameroon) in 1984 (In minutes per day at three different periods of the year)

	Small dry season (July–August)					Rainy season (November–December)					Dry season (March–April)				
	Women	%	Men	%	Women/ Men	Women	%	Men	%	Women/ Men	Women	%	Men	%	Women/ Men
Sleeping	598	41.6%	537	37.3%	111.4%	581	40.4%	489	34.0%	118.8%	575	40.0%	505	35.1%	113.9%
Personal care	190	13.2%	302	21.0%	62.9%	210	14.6%	310	21.5%	67.7%	189	13.1%	341	23.7%	55.4%
Care of children	7	0.5%	11	0.8%	63.6%	23	1.6%	10	0.7%	230.0%	13	0.9%	12	0.8%	108.3%
Household duties	484	33.6%	28	1.9%	1728.6%	429	29.8%	49	3.4%	875.5%	410	28.5%	62	4.3%	661.3%
Agriculture	75	5.2%	28	1.9%	267.9%	71	4.9%	38	2.6%	186.8%	127	8.8%	64	4.4%	198.4%
Fishing	8	0.6%	131	9.1%	6.1%	25	1.7%	240	16.7%	10.4%	19	1.3%	195	13.5%	9.7%
Hunting	0	0.0%	20	1.4%	0.0%	0	0.0%	17	1.2%	0.0%	0	0.0%	2	0.1%	0.0%
Construction	0	0.0%	115	8.0%	0.0%	0	0.0%	3	0.2%	0.0%	0	0.0%	20	1.4%	0.0%
Social activities	77	5.4%	268	18.6%	28.7%	100	6.9%	283	19.7%	35.3%	106	7.4%	239	16.6%	44.4%
Total	1439	100.0%	1440	100.0%	99.9%	1439	100.0%	1439	100.0%	100.0%	1439	100.0%	1440	100.0%	99.9%
Total work SNA	83	5.8%	294	20.4%	28.2%	96	6.7%	298	20.7%	32.2%	146	10.1%	281	19.5%	52.0%
Total work	574	39.9%	333	23.1%	172.4%	548	38.1%	357	24.8%	153.5%	569	39.5%	355	24.7%	160.3%

Source: Based on data from Pasquet and Koppert (1993 and 1996).

Table 3.15. Time Use among the Mvae of Campo (Southwest Cameroon) in 1984 in minutes per day at three different periods of the year)

	Small dry season (July–August)		Rainy season (November–December)		Dry season (March–April)				Women/ Men
	Women	%	Women	%	Women	%	Men	%	Men
Sleeping	642	44.6%	646	44.9%	595	41.3%	633	44.0%	94.0%
Personal care	158	11.0%	215	14.9%	207	14.4%	399	27.7%	51.9%
Care of children	5	0.3%	18	1.3%	15	1.0%	15	1.0%	100.0%
Household duties	375	26.1%	334	23.2%	273	19.0%	63	4.4%	433.3%
Agriculture	197	13.7%	91	6.3%	250	17.4%	148	10.3%	168.9%
Fishing	14	1.0%	63	4.4%	23	1.6%	18	1.3%	127.8%
Hunting	12	0.8%	2	0.1%	25	1.7%	66	4.6%	37.9%
Construction	0	0.0%	1	0.1%	0	0.0%	10	0.7%	0.0%
Social activities	36	2.5%	70	4.9%	52	3.6%	88	6.1%	59.1%
Total	1439	100.0%	1440	100.0%	1440	100.0%	1440	100.0%	100.0%
Total work SNA	223	15.5%	157	10.9%	298	20.7%	242	16.8%	123.1%
Total work	603	41.9%	509	35.3%	586	40.7%	320	22.2%	183.1%

Source: Based on data from Pasquet and Koppert (1993 and 1996).

than for men (from 20 to 21 percent). The total time spent on work ranges from 38 to 40 percent for women and from 23 to 25 percent for men, a level much higher than in the recent time use surveys.

Time Use Patterns and Key Development Variables

The results of time use surveys, which have been presented and analyzed in a previous section are based on the entire sample population (aged 6 or 10 to 65 or more) or on the population engaged in the referenced activities. Provided that demographic and socio-economic characteristics of the respondents have been collected, the reports of the surveys also give time use patterns by age group, by educational level, by region or province. They can also give them by marital status (single, married, polygamous, divorced), by type of activity status (active, inactive), employment status (own-account worker, wage earner, contributing family worker), occupational status, and so forth. The South African survey also collected the income group and the source of income. The Benin and Madagascar surveys cross-classify urban/rural areas, provinces, active/inactive, 6–14 attending

Table 3.16. Comparisons of Daily Time Use for Women and Men in Four Sub-Saharan African Countries (In percent of a 24-hour day)

Activities	South Africa 2000			Benin 1998			Madagascar 2001			Mauritius (2003)		
	Women	Men	Both Sexes	Women	Men	Both Sexes	Women	Men	Both Sexes	Women	Men	Both Sexes
SNA activities	7.8%	12.8%	10.1%	16.4%	16.3%	16.2%	11.7%	19.3%	15.4%	8.4%	21.4%	14.9%
Domestic and care activities	14.6%	5.7%	10.4%	13.6%	4.2%	9.0%	15.1%	3.7%	9.7%	18.6%	5.3%	12.8%
Work	22.4%	18.5%	20.5%	30.0%	20.5%	25.2%	26.8%	22.9%	25.1%	28.5%	26.7%	27.6%
School, studying	6.4%	7.4%	6.7%	4.5%	7.6%	6.2%	6.4%	7.6%	7.0%	4.7%	4.9%	4.8%
Social activities	8.8%	9.4%	9.1%	5.9%	8.0%	7.2%	2.3%	2.7%	2.3%	7.6%	10.7%	9.1%
Leisure	8.5%	10.4%	9.4%	3.8%	6.9%	5.2%	9.0%	10.6%	9.7%	7.8%	7.3%	7.6%
Commuting	4.1%	5.7%	5.1%	2.1%	3.5%	3.1%	2.7%	4.0%	3.3%	0.0%	0.0%	0.0%
Sleeping, eating, resting, personal care	49.8%	48.7%	49.2%	53.7%	53.5%	53.1%	52.8%	52.2%	52.5%	51.4%	50.4%	50.9%
Total	100.0%	100.0%	100.0%	100.0%	100.0%	100.0%	100.0%	100.0%	100.0%	100.0%	100.0%	100.0%

Source: See sources for Table 3.13.

Table 3.17. Time Use among the Yassa of Campo (Southwest Cameroon) in 1984
(In minutes per day at three different periods of the year;
in percent of a 24-hour day)

	Small dry season (July–August)			Rainy season (November–December)			Dry season (March–April)		
	Women	Men	Women/ Men	Women	Men	Women/ Men	Women	Men	Women/ Men
SNA activities	5.8%	20.4%	28.2%	6.7%	20.7%	32.2%	10.1%	19.5%	52.0%
Domestic and care activities	34.1%	2.7%	1728.6%	31.4%	4.1%	875.5%	29.4%	5.1%	661.3%
Work	39.9%	23.1%	172.4%	38.1%	24.8%	153.5%	39.5%	24.7%	160.3%
Social activities	5.4%	18.6%	28.7%	6.9%	19.7%	35.3%	7.4%	16.6%	44.4%
Sleeping, Personal care	54.8%	58.3%	94.0%	55.0%	55.5%	99.1%	53.1%	58.8%	90.3%
Total	100.0%	100.0%	99.9%	100.0%	100.0%	100.0%	100.0%	100.0%	99.9%

Source: See sources for Table 3.14.

school/not attending school, household heads/wives, wives of polygamous, unmarried women, wage earners and own-account workers. An example of comparative results by province is provided for Madagascar (see Tables 3.A1 and 3.A2 in annex).

As a matter of fact, descriptive statistical tables do not show much difference in time use patterns for most of these categories, except at a provincial level. Analytical research could be undertaken in order to highlight those behaviors.

However, it is certainly possible to go further. The Madagascar survey was carried out as a parallel sample of the continuous living standards surveys and the Mauritius survey was part of a multi-purpose household survey. The Benin survey was also part of a continuous household survey. The Ghana survey is part of the living standard survey. The ongoing time use survey of Tunisia (2005) is a subsample of the Budget-Consumption household survey. Therefore, a direct outcome of these surveys should be the presentation of the time use patterns by socio-economic category of the household.

The socio-economic categories of households used in living standards surveys generally identify the categories through the household heads. They distinguish among them the subsistence farmers (or rather food crop farmers), the export crop farmers, the public wage earners, the private wage earners, the non-agricultural employers, the own-account workers in trade, the own-account workers in other non-agricultural activities, the inactive or unemployed, and so forth. Households can also be categorized, for instance according to the number of children under age 6, type of access to water and source of energy, the distance to main services (transport, health, schools), the type of technology used, and so forth.

Until now no official household survey has collected information on the presence of an HIV/AIDS infected household member within the household. Even the Demographic and Health Surveys (DHS) regularly conducted in most African countries have limited their investigation in this domain to questions of opinion and awareness about the infection and the means to protect from it. Therefore, it does not seem possible to measure the impact of HIV/AIDS on time use. A possible solution could be to ask a question on sickness in general without detailing the kind of sickness. It has already been stressed that caring for adults takes three times more time in South Africa than in the four other countries, which seems to be an indication of a correlation with the presence of the infection.

All the usual cross-classifications of income-expenditure/budget-consumption surveys would be interesting to tabulate with respect to time use patterns of the household members: income groups of the household, expenditure group, extremely poor/poor/nonpoor. At least the Madagascar, Benin, and Ghana surveys, and possibly Mauritius, could be revisited for more in-depth analyses of micro-data. It would allow looking at the variations and trends in time use patterns in relation to the income (or expenditure) groups for assessing the impact of poverty in monetary terms, and in relation to access to services for assessing the impact of human poverty, and finally assessing the impact of time poverty.

Given the scarce number of data usable for capturing trends, it may be important to better analyze structural changes in time use across income or occupational groups, socio-economic categories and types of access to drinking water in order to highlight for instance the shifting of time from fetching water or wood to care of children or to paid work, depending on the category of household.

Moreover the African Gender and Development Centre (ACGD) of the UN Economic Commission for Africa has embarked into a five-year programme, an outcome of which is an Africa-specific Guidebook for Mainstreaming Gender Perspectives and Household Production in National Planning Instruments and Policies (Charmes 2003a and 2003b; UNECA, 2005). This compendium of tools and methodologies for time use surveys in particular is going to be applied in several African countries where continuous time use surveys will be implemented. It could be a good opportunity to systematize the analysis of time use surveys in terms of time poverty.

Measuring and Analyzing Time Poverty

Feminization of poverty has become a major challenge for economic theory and development policies since the middle of the 1990s and the 1995 Beijing Conference when it was put on the forefront as an important issue to be tackled. Since then it has played the role of a powerful slogan in parallel with the recognition that "if not engendered, development is endangered."

Illustrating and demonstrating the so-called feminization of poverty has remained, however, a challenge for scholars and researchers given that empirical evidence of gender inequalities within the household does not exist (or only scarcely and on not very sound and representative bases). Poverty is measured through household income and expenditures and, if sources of income and expenditures can be recorded individually, it is far more difficult to know how they have been spent or consumed on an individual basis, especially food consumption. Consequently, income poverty cannot easily be used to prove the feminization of poverty except that there are more and more female-headed households that are poor. The gender distribution of males and females within the female-headed and male-headed households being equal, it is not possible to deduct from this observation that the number of women in poverty is increasing.

Given the difficulties arising from the income poverty approach, another dimension of poverty was analyzed: access to services, included in what is called "human poverty." Yet, unless the gender distribution of frequentation of health services or other types of services is available as a regular statistical indicator, this approach is also difficult to analyze in a gender perspective because all household members are supposed to be equal with respect to the distance to the services. This is not true in terms of time because access to services, access to water in particular—and the duty of fetching water (or collecting fuel) for instance—are typically feminine tasks. This is why the human poverty approach inevitably leads to another dimension of poverty, which is "time poverty."

The time poverty approach is recent and encompasses the strict dimension of access to services. Women are poorer than men in terms of time because they must systematically add up domestic and care duties (reproductive work) to their market or non-market productive work so that this double time-budget makes of time a resource which is more scarce for women than for men. Therefore, policies oriented toward an alleviation of female time budgets can have major impacts on resources derived from income generating activities due to an increased amount of time dedicated to them, or also on children's health thanks to an increased amount of time dedicated to care. There are naturally some domestic activities or SNA non-market activities toward which efforts should be concentrated in order to spare time that could be devoted to more gainful or productive work: fetching water and firewood are typically such activities to be spared, as well as commuting.

The time poverty approach thus opens new horizons for policy purposes. More in-depth analyses of existing surveys are necessary to provide sound and convincing arguments to policymakers. This is the task ahead of us.

References

Charmes J. 1989. "Trente cinq ans de comptabilité nationale du secteur informel au Burkina Faso (1954-89). Leçons d'une expérience et perspectives d'amélioration." Ministère du Plan et de la Coopération, PNUD-DTCD, rapport n° 13C, Ouagadougou.

———. 2000. "African Women in Food Processing: A Major, But Still Underestimated Sector of Their Contribution to the National Economy." IDRC, Ottawa, Nairobi.

———. 2003a. "Application of Time Use to Assess the Contribution of Women to GDP and to Monitor Impacts of National Budget on Women's Time Use." Expert Group Meeting on a Gender-Aware Macroeconomic Model to Evaluate Impacts of Policies on Poverty Reduction, May 7–9, Addis Ababa, Ethiopia. United nations Economic Commission for Africa African Centre for Gender and Development.

———. 2003b. "Easy Reference Guide on Tools for Mainstreaming Gender in Poverty Reduction Strategies: National Accounts, National Budgets and Time Use Studies." United Nations Economic Commission for Africa, African Centre for Gender and Development (ACGD), Addis Ababa.

————. 2005. "Femmes africaines, activités économiques et travail: de l'invisibilité à la reconnaissance." *Revue Tiers Monde* 46(182):255–279.

Charmes, J., and Jeemol Unni. 2004. "Measurement of Work." In G. Standing and M. Chen eds., *Reconceptualising Work*. Geneva: ILO.

Geslin, P. 1997. "L'innovation et le temps. Une approche ethnographique de la réallocation du temps de travail agricole chez les Soussou de Guinée." In C. Blanc-Pamard and J. Boutrais, eds. *Dynamique des systèmes agraires: Nouvelles recherches rurales au Sud.* Paris: ORSTOM

Ghana Statistical Service. 1995. "Ghana Living Standards Survey, Report of the 3rd Round (GLSS 3), September 1991–September 1992." Accra.

————. 2000. "Ghana Living Standards Survey, Report of the 4th Round (GLSS 4)." Accra.

INSAE/PNUD. 1998. *Enquête emploi du temps au Bénin, Méthodologie et résultats.* Cotonou.

INSTAT. 2002. *EPM 2001. Module Emploi du Temps.* Antananarivo: INSTAT- DSM/PNUD-MAG/97/007.

Leplaideur, A. 1978. *Les travaux agricoles chez les paysans du Centre-Sud Cameroun, les techniques utilisées et les temps nécessaires.* Paris: IRAT.

Pasquet, P., and G. Koppert. 1993. "Activity Patterns and Energy Expenditure in Cameroonian Tropical Forest Populations." In C.M. Hladik, A. Hladik, O.F. Linares, H. Pagezy, A. Semple, and M. Hadley, *Tropical Forests, People and Food. Biocultural Interactions and Applications to Development.* Man and the Biosphere Series, 13. Paris: UNESCO and Carnforth, The Parthenon Publishing Group.

————. 1996. "Budget-temps et dépense énergétique chez les essarteurs forestiers du Cameroun." In C.M. Hladik, A. Hladik, H. Pagezy, O.F. Linares, G. Koppert, and A. Froment, eds., *L'alimentation en forêt tropicale: Interactions bioculturelles et perspectives de développement.* L'Homme et la Biosphère, Editions. Paris: UNESCO.

Republic of Mauritius, Central Statistics Office. 2004. "Continuous Multi-Purpose Household Survey 2003, Main results of the time use study." Port Louis.

SNA. 1993. System of National Accounts, Commission of the European Communities, IMF, OECD, UN, WB.

Statistics South Africa. 2001. *A Survey of Time Use. How South African Women and Men Spend Their Time.* Pretoria.

United Nations Economic Commission for Africa. 2005. *A Guidebook for Mainstreaming Gender Perspectives and Household Production into National Statistics, Budgets and Policies in Africa.* African Centre for Gender and Development. Addis Ababa.

Whittington D., M. Winming, and R. Roche. 1990. "Calculating the Value of Time Spent Collecting Water: Some Estimates for Ukunda, Kenya." *World Development* 18(2): 269–280.

Appendix Table 3.A1. Time Use Patterns for Household Members from 6 to 65 Years Old in Urban Areas by Province (Faritany), Sex, and Activity (In percent of the total number of hours per day)

		Antananarivo	Fianarantsoa	Toamasina	Mahajanga	Toliara	Antsiranana	Madagascar
WOMEN	SNA market production	9.2	9.2	8.0	10.5	6.8	7.5	8.7
	SNA non market production	2.5	5.2	4.7	2.9	4.7	2.6	3.4
	Non-SNA production: Domestic, care	16.5	16.5	14.8	14.7	14.7	13.9	15.6
	School	7.5	4.4	5.4	5.6	6.4	8.6	6.5
	Social activities	2.7	2.5	2.3	2.5	2.3	2.2	2.5
	Leisure	10.6	9.4	8.8	7.6	7.8	8.5	9.3
	Travel	3.0	1.9	3.0	3.0	2.0	4.0	2.8
	Sleeping, resting, eating, personal care	52.1	56.5	56.8	55.3	57.2	52.6	54.7
	Total	100.0 (25h)	100.0 (25.4h)	100.0 (24.9h)	100.0 (24.5h)	100.0 (24.5h)	100.0 (24.0h)	100.0 (24.9h)
MEN	SNA market production	17.7	14.7	16.4	16.1	14.1	15.3	16.3
	SNA non market production	2.5	7.0	4.6	4.5	5.5	2.2	3.8
	Non-SNA production: Domestic, care	4.2	3.7	3.7	3.7	2.7	5.0	3.9
	School	8.6	7.2	6.5	6.4	9.0	8.1	7.8
	Social activities	3.0	2.8	2.9	2.9	1.7	2.6	2.7
	Leisure	13.0	9.6	8.0	7.9	10.0	10.1	11.0
	Travel	4.3	3.5	4.7	4.6	4.0	5.3	4.3
	Sleeping, resting, eating, personal care	51.4	56.2	57.1	56.1	55.1	51.6	54.4
	Total	100.0 (25.1h)	100.0 (25.1h)	100.0 (24.9h)	100.0 (24.5h)	100.0 (24.5h)	100.0 (24.1h)	100.0 (25.0h)

(continued)

Appendix Table 3.A1. Time Use Patterns for Household Members from 6 to 65 Years Old in Urban Areas by Province (Faritany), Sex, and Activity (In percent of the total number of hours per day) (Continued)

	Antananarivo	Fianarantsoa	Toamasina	Mahajanga	Toliara	Antsiranana	Madagascar
BOTH SEXES							
SNA market production	13.2	11.7	12.6	13.2	10.4	10.5	12.3
SNA non market production	2.5	6.0	4.3	3.7	5.1	2.4	3.6
Non-SNA production: Domestic, care	10.5	10.8	9.2	9.3	8.7	10.4	10.1
School	8.0	5.7	5.7	6.0	7.7	8.4	7.2
Social activities	2.9	2.7	2.2	2.6	2.0	2.3	2.6
Leisure	11.8	9.5	10.0	7.7	8.9	9.2	10.2
Travel	3.6	2.6	3.9	3.8	3.0	4.5	3.5
Sleeping, resting, eating, personal care	51.7	56.5	56.0	55.5	56.1	52.3	54.7
Total	100.0 (25h)	100.0 (25.3h)	100.0 (24.9h)	100.0 (24.4)	100.0 (24.5h)	100.0 (24.1h)	100.0 (25.0h)

Note: One percentage point is approximately equivalent to 15 minutes. The total number of hours per day exceeds 24 because of simultaneous activities.
Source: INSTAT (2002), EPM 2001. Module Emploi du Temps, Antananarivo, INSTAT- DSM/PNUD-MAG/97/007.

Appendix Table 3.A2. Time Use Patterns for Household Members from 6 to 65 Years Old in Rural Areas by Province (Faritany), Sex, and Activity (In percent of the total number of hours per day)

		Antananarivo	Fianarantsoa	Toamasina	Mahajanga	Toliara	Antsiranana	Madagascar
WOMEN	SNA market production	10.2	8.7	7.5	5.0	6.6	8.0	8.1
	SNA non market production	6.8	8.8	8.1	10.0	12.0	7.6	8.7
	Non-SNA production: Domestic, care	15.5	13.5	13.7	17.2	13.5	13.8	14.6
	School	5.8	4.1	2.9	2.1	3.8	3.4	4.0
	Social activities	1.2	3.2	3.0	2.8	1.5	3.4	2.3
	Leisure	5.7	5.3	5.3	6.8	4.9	4.0	5.4
	Travel	2.8	1.9	2.8	1.8	1.3	2.1	2.1
	Sleeping, resting, eating, personal care	54.0	58.0	59.3	55.9	57.2	57.6	56.9
	Total	100.0 (24.5h)	100.0 (24.8h)	100.0 (24.6h)	100.0 (24.4h)	100.0 (24.2h)	100.0 (24.0h)	100.0 (24.5h)
MEN	SNA market production	17.7	14.1	13.9	12.2	15.4	11.9	14.80
	SNA non market production	7.6	9.9	9.9	12.5	13.8	10.6	10.2
	Non-SNA production: Domestic, care	2.9	2.2	3.1	3.2	2.0	2.4	2.7
	School	5.7	4.6	2.7	1.6	2.7	4.2	3.9
	Social activities	1.9	3.8	4.0	4.0	1.8	2.6	3.0
	Leisure	8.0	7.4	5.1	7.2	6.4	7.3	7.0
	Travel	3.7	3.9	4.4	3.8	2.7	3.9	3.7
	Sleeping, resting, eating, personal care	54.8	57.9	59.2	57.0	56.0	57.0	56.9
	Total	100.0 (24.5h)	100.0 (24.9h)	100.0 (24.6h)	100.0 (24.4h)	100.0 (24.2h)	100.0 (24.0h)	100.0 (24.5h)

(continued)

Appendix Table 3.A2. Time Use Patterns for Household Members from 6 to 65 Years Old in Rural Areas by Province (Faritany), Sex, and Activity (In percent of the total number of hours per day) (Continued)

		Antananarivo	Fianarantsoa	Toamasina	Mahajanga	Toliara	Antsiranana	Madagascar
BOTH SEXES	SNA market production	13.9	11.3	10.6	10.6	8.5	10.8	9.9
	SNA non market production	7.2	9.3	9.0	9.0	11.2	12.8	9.1
	Non-SNA production: Domestic, care	9.2	8.1	8.6	8.6	10.4	8.1	8.3
	School	5.7	4.3	2.8	2.8	1.9	3.3	3.8
	Social activities	1.5	3.5	3.5	3.5	3.5	1.7	3.0
	Leisure	6.8	6.2	5.2	5.2	7.0	5.6	5.6
	Travel	3.2	2.9	3.6	3.6	2.7	1.9	3.0
	Sleeping, resting, eating, personal care	54.4	57.9	59.2	59.2	56.5	56.6	57.5
	Total	100.0 (24.5h)	100.0 (24.8h)	100.0 (24.6h)	100.0 (24.4h)	100.0 (24.2h)	100.0 (24.1h)	100.0 (25.0h)

Note: One percentage point is approximately equivalent to 15 minutes. The total number of hours per day exceeds 24 because of simultaneous activities.

Source: INSTAT (2002), EPM 2001. Module Emploi du Temps, Antananarivo, INSTAT- DSM/PNUD-MAG/97/007.

PART II

Measuring Time Poverty

Measuring Time Poverty and Analyzing Its Determinants: Concepts and Application to Guinea

Elena Bardasi and Quentin Wodon[11]

The availability of better data on time use in developing countries makes it important to provide tools for analyzing such data. While the idea of "time poverty" is not new, and while many papers have provided measures of time use and hinted at the concept of time poverty, we have not seen in the literature formal discussions and measurement of the concept of time poverty alongside the techniques used for measuring consumption poverty. Conceptually, time poverty can be understood as the fact that some individuals do not have enough time for rest and leisure after taking into account the time spent working, whether in the labor market, for domestic work, or for other activities such as fetching water and wood. Unlike consumption or income, where economists assume that "more is better," time is a limited resource—more time spent working in paid or unpaid work-related activities means less leisure, and therefore higher "time poverty." Our aim in this paper is to provide a simple application of the concepts used in the consumption poverty literature to time use, in order to obtain measures of time poverty for a population as a whole and for various groups of individuals.

There has been an increase in interest in recent years in analytical work on the economic analysis of time use (see for example the papers in Hamermesh and Pfann 2005). The allocation of time has implications in a wide range of areas, as illustrated

11. The authors are with the World Bank. This work was prepared as a contribution to the Poverty Assessment for Guinea prepared at the World Bank. The authors acknowledge support from the Trust Fund ESSDD as well as the Belgian Poverty Reduction Partnership for research on this issue as part of a small research program on gender, time use and poverty in Sub-Saharan Africa which also benefited from funding from the GENFUND. Preliminary results from the paper were presented at a three-day workshop organized in Guinea in October 2005 in collaboration with the country's National Statistical Office (*Direction Nationale de la Statistique*), and at a World Bank workshop in November 2005. We are grateful to Kathleen Beegle and Mark Blackden for comments. The views expressed here are those of the authors and need not reflect those of the World Bank, its Executive Directors or the countries they represent.

for example by work on transportation (Zhang, Timmermans, and Borgers 2005) and taxation (Apps and Rees 2004). In developing countries, the issue of time use has been discussed in relationship among others to the ability of household members to increase their supply of labor (Newman 2002), given strict time constraints due among others to limited access to basic infrastructure services. The role of illness in limiting the ability of women to take advantage of economic opportunities due to the burden of care has also been highlighted (Ilahi 2000 and 2001). A broader discussion of the implications of time use issues for growth and development is available in the report "Engendering Development" by the World Bank (2001; see also Blackden and Bhanu 1999; Gelb 2001; Apps 2004).

The importance of time use stems in part from the understanding that the welfare of individuals and households is a function not solely of their income or consumption, but also of their freedom in allocating time. Clearly, time use allocation and constraints, especially as they relate to labor markets, have implications for the ability of households to escape poverty. For example, Vickery (1977) argued that reaching the minimal level of consumption used for poverty measurement in the United States requires both money and time, which matters when designing income transfer programs. More generally, in their review of the literature on time use prepared for the World Bank's manual on Living Standard Measurement Surveys, Harvey and Taylor (2000) argue that households need a minimum number of hours—the "household time overhead" concept—to complete domestic chores, with a lower such overhead leading to higher levels of welfare.

In Sub-Saharan Africa, the issue of time use is especially important because of the high workload carried by many and the relationship between time use and consumption poverty. Households have a high probability of being consumption poor, so that any opportunity to enable them to make a better livelihood, for example by shifting time from low- to high-productivity activities should be pursued. Furthermore, time use issues have strong gender dimensions, as African women often have to work long hours for domestic chores and the collection of water and wood apart from working in the fields or in other productive occupations.

On the data front, time use surveys have been implemented for many years in several developed countries, but in developing countries, their use had been more limited so far, with much of the evidence coming from small-scale village-level instruments or otherwise small samples. Recently, thanks to efforts by the United Nations' statistics division, nationally representative time use surveys have been carried in India and Nepal in 1999, Benin in 1998, Nigeria in 1999, South Africa in 2000, Madagascar in 2001, and Mauritius in 2003. The results from these surveys are reviewed by Charmes (see Chapter 3). In addition, time use data have also been available in a range of other surveys similar to the Living Standards Measurement Surveys (LSMS) promoted by the World Bank. In Sub-Saharan Africa, examples of recent LSMS-type surveys with time use modules include Ghana in 1991–92 and 1998-99, Guinea in 2002–03, Malawi in 2004, Mauritania in 2000, and Sierra Leone in 2003. This is by no means an exhaustive list, but it does indicate that more data are becoming available to conduct work on these issues. In the Unites States as well, in recognition of the importance of better analytical work on time use issues, a new time use survey is being implemented (Hamermesh, Frazis, and Stewart 2005).

The availability of better data for time use analysis in developing countries makes it important to provide tools for analyzing such data. While the idea of "time poverty" is not new, and while many papers have provided measures of time use and hinted at the concept of time poverty, we have not seen in the literature much formal discussion and measurement of the concept of time poverty alongside the techniques used for measuring consumption poverty. Conceptually, time poverty can be understood as the fact that some individuals do not have enough time for rest and leisure after taking into account the time spent working, whether in the labor market, for domestic work, or for other activities such as fetching water and wood. Another way to consider the issue of time poverty is to argue that individuals who are extremely pressed for time are not able to allocate sufficient time for important activities, and are therefore forced to make difficult tradeoffs. The analogy with consumption poverty would be a household that, because of insufficient income, would need to sacrifice some key basic needs in order to be able to afford other basic needs. However, unlike consumption or income, of which economists assume that "more is better," time is a limited resource—more time spent working in paid or unpaid productive activities means less leisure, and therefore higher "time poverty." Our aim in this paper is then to provide a simple application of the concepts used in the consumption poverty literature to time use, in order to obtain measures of time poverty for a population as a whole and for various groups of individuals.

Because there is less consensus on the benefits and costs of time spent working than on the value of a higher consumption or income level for households, the very concept of time poverty may be challenged. For example, can we consider as time poor relatively wealthy individuals or households whose members work longer hours in order to achieve higher levels of income or satisfaction at work? We would argue that time poverty would apply to such individuals, because long working hours will indeed reduce the time available for leisure, rest, or friends and family. This does not mean that time poor individuals are worse off than other individuals—simply, time poverty is one of the many dimensions that may affect an individual's level of welfare and satisfaction with life.

Another question relates to the treatment of those who are not time poor in the measurement of time poverty. It is important to realize that all poverty measures are censored variables. That is, for consumption or income poverty, only those below the monetary poverty line affect the consumption poverty measure, while the individuals above the monetary threshold are assigned a value of zero for their contribution to aggregate consumption poverty. Similarly for time poverty, only those above the time poverty line affect the time poverty measure, while the individuals below the time poverty line are assigned a value of zero for their contribution to aggregate time poverty. This means that by considering in the time poverty measure only those individuals who work more hours than the time poverty line, the measure is itself silent on the situation of the non-time poor, apart from asserting that they are not time poor. In other words, no assumptions are made in terms of comparing the welfare in the time use dimension of those individuals who work, say, 40 hours versus 20 hours per week.

We would argue that precisely because it would be difficult to make comparisons of time use welfare between individuals who are within the normal range of work hours—some may prefer to work 20 hours while others may prefer to work 40 hours, the time poverty concept is the right one to use for the analysis because it does not require such comparisons of time-based welfare below a threshold that would be sufficiently high so as to ensure that tradeoffs have to be made by individuals above that threshold. Said differently, the fact that poverty measures are censored makes such measures especially well adapted to the analysis of time poverty by considering only in the measures those who are time poor and not requiring any specific assumption for the comparison of working hours among individuals who are not time poor.

Still another question is whether individuals are really time constrained, or whether, for almost all individuals, there would be an ability to work more, in which case the concept of time poverty would be for practical purposes mostly irrelevant. This is an empirical question, but evidence does suggest the presence of upper bounds on working time for individuals. For example, using data from Ecuador, Newman (2002) shows that when women took advantage of new labor market opportunities in the cut flower industry, their total labor time remained constant, so that men had to provide higher amounts of work in unpaid tasks. The analysis of seasonality in time use in Malawi provided in this volume by Wodon and Beegle (Chapter 5) also suggests that there may be labor scarcity at crucial periods of the year despite underemployment in many other periods. These examples suggest that the concept of time poverty is a potentially important one. In the rest of this paper, after outlining our analytical framework in the next section, we present empirical results obtained with a recent survey for Guinea on the extent of time poverty in that country. A brief conclusion follows.

Analytical Framework

This paper provides measures of time poverty in Guinea using the latest nationally representative household survey for the period 2002–2003. Our framework is straightforward as we simply apply the traditional concepts and techniques used for the analysis of income or consumption poverty to time poverty. For the reader who may not be familiar with these concepts, we follow their presentation as provided by Coudouel, Hentschel, and Wodon (2002), and simply adapt this presentation to the measurement of time poverty.

In most empirical research on poverty, poverty measures of the so-called FGT class (Foster, Greer, and Thorbecke 1984) are used. The first three measures of this class are the headcount index of poverty, the poverty gap, and the squared poverty gap. In a time poverty framework, the headcount index is the share of the population which is time poor, that is, the proportion of the population that works a number of hours y that is above a certain time poverty line z. Suppose we have a population of size n in which q individuals are time poor. Then the headcount index of time poverty is defined as:

$$H = \frac{q}{n} \qquad (1)$$

The time poverty gap represents the mean distance separating the population from the time poverty line, with the non-time poor being given a distance of zero. This measures the time deficit of the entire population, in effect, the amount of time that would be needed to shift all individuals who are time poor below a given time poverty line through perfectly targeted "time transfers." Such transfers are actually provided to some households in some developed countries, for example through the provision of subsidies for taking care of children in working families (or simply of large families—in Belgium, households having three very young children may benefit from the help of a social worker at home.) Mathematically, the time poverty gap is defined as follows:

$$PG = \frac{1}{n} \sum_{i=1}^{q} \left[\frac{y_i - z}{z} \right] \tag{2}$$

where y_i is total working hours of individual i, and the sum is taken only among those individuals who are time poor. Consider for example a situation in which the time poverty gap is equal to 0.20. This means that the transfer of time needed to enable all time-poor individuals to escape time poverty represents 20 percent of the time poverty line on average. If the total time available (say, after accounting for a minimum amount of time devoted to rest) is equal to twice the time poverty line, the time transfer that would be needed to eradicate time poverty would represent 10 percent of the total time available. Such simple calculations can be used to communicate in an intuitive manner the meaning of the time poverty gap and the magnitude of the time reallocation that would be needed in order to eradicate time poverty. In practice however, given that perfectly-targeted time transfers to eradicate time poverty are neither feasible nor necessarily a good thing, one must be careful in their use. Note also that the time poverty gap can be written as being equal to the product of the headcount index of time poverty by the time gap ratio I, i.e. $PG = H * I$, with I itself defined as:

$$I = \frac{y_q - z}{z} \text{ where } y_q = \frac{1}{q} \sum_{i=1}^{q} y_i \text{ is the mean working hours of the time poor.} \tag{3}$$

As is well known in the poverty literature, the time gap ratio I is not a good measure of poverty in itself, because there may be situations where the time gap ratio is reduced over time. For example, if some individuals who are close to the time poverty line reduce their working hours, they may escape time poverty, so that aggregate time poverty as measured by the time poverty gap would be reduced, but with an increase in the time gap ratio computed among those individuals who remain time poor.

While the time poverty gap takes into account the distance separating the time poor from the time poverty line, the squared time poverty gap takes the square of that distance into account. When using the squared time poverty gap, more weight is given to those who have extra long working hours. Said differently, the squared poverty gap takes into account the inequality among the time poor. It is defined as:

$$SPG = \frac{1}{n} \sum_{i=1}^{q} \left[\frac{y_i - z}{z} \right]^2 \tag{4}$$

The headcount, poverty gap, and squared poverty gap are the FGT class of poverty measures whose formula includes a parameter α taking a value of zero for the headcount, one for the poverty gap, and two for the squared poverty gap in the following expression:

$$P\alpha = \frac{1}{n} \sum_{i=1}^{q} \left[\frac{y_i - z}{z} \right]^{\alpha} \tag{5}$$

In terms of interpretation, it is worth noting that contrary to what happens with monetary poverty measures, the (normalized) time poverty gap need not always be smaller than the time headcount index, and the squared time poverty gap need not be smaller than the time poverty gap. When using $(z - y)/z$ as the household level indicator for consumption or income poverty, the normalization of $(z - y)$ by z implies that we always have values that are between zero and one. For time poverty by contrast, because the definition in (5) relies instead on the value of $(y - z)/z$, we may have relatively large values for $y - z$, so that some values at the individual level may be larger than one, and the poverty gap may itself have a higher value than the headcount index in the aggregate, especially if the time poverty line is set at a relatively low value. However, as long as one remembers that the division by z is only used for normalization purpose, so that it does not affect the key properties that poverty measures must observe, this should not lead to confusion. In case of confusion, it would suffice to use an alternative normalization, such as $(y - z)/168$ if we are using weekly hours as the benchmark (because there are 168 hours in a week), in order to make sure that all the time poverty measures are between zero and one.

A few more comments may be useful before presenting an empirical illustration. Firstly, when measuring time poverty, we have data at the individual level, while in most cases, when measuring income or consumption poverty, we only have aggregate data at the household level. This means that for time poverty, we can look at intra-household allocations and at the impact of intra-household time inequality on time poverty.

Secondly, there is always a difficulty in traditional poverty measurement in comparing the welfare of households of different sizes and composition, because of differences in needs between individuals, as well as economies of scale in consumption. To some extent, these difficulties persist for the measurement of time poverty, as there may be differences in needs for time poverty measurement, for example if children need more rest and leisure time than adults. By contrast, even though there are clearly economies of scale at the household level in terms of the amount of time required to perform some domestic tasks that benefit all household members at once, this is not problematic for the measurement of time use because we observe the hours of work of each individual.

Thirdly, although (1) to (3) above are written by considering the amount of work above a certain time poverty threshold, they could be modified to consider instead as time poor those individuals who have less than a certain amount of time for leisure and rest. This can be done because the amount of time available in one day is fixed, so that there is a perfect correspondence between the two approaches. If the amount of time available in a day were not bounded, we would need to use the "above the line" approach both for measurement and for assessments of the robustness time poverty comparisons, as done in the case of pollution and CO_2 emissions by Makdissi and Wodon (2004).

Fourthly, what is perhaps more arbitrary when analyzing time poverty as compared to consumption poverty is the choice of the time poverty line above which individuals are considered as overworked or time poor, and thereby lacking enough time for leisure and rest. In the income/consumption poverty literature, we often have clear nutritional-based "cost of basic needs" approaches to estimating poverty lines. When dealing with time poverty, the correct level for the time poverty line is less clear, at least if one wants to consider an allocation of time for leisure on top of what is strictly needed for rest from a health point of view. In practice, depending on the social context of the country for which the analysis is conducted, we may want to use relative as opposed to absolute time poverty lines together with some tests for the robustness of comparisons of time poverty obtained over time or across households groups to the choice of the time poverty line.

Data and Results

Time Use Statistics

To illustrate time poverty measurement and comparisons, we use data from Guinea for the year 2002–2003. The data are from the EIBEP (*Enquête Intégrale de Base pour l'Evaluation de la Pauvreté*) survey implemented between October 2002 and October 2003 by the *Direction nationale de la statistique* (DNS) of the Ministry of Planning. The individual-level indicator that we use to determine who is time poor is the total amount of time spent by individuals working, whether in the labor market, in domestic chores or in collecting water and wood. Note that we have no information about the time spent caring for children, sick household members and disabled people. This probably leads us to underestimate the workload of individuals, even if we could argue that this activity is often performed as a "secondary activity" in combination with one of the other productive or domestic activities recorded in the questionnaire and included in our estimates of the total time devoted to work. We also create a second definition of the total time allocated to work by adding to the components of the first definition the amount of time spent helping other households and in community services (this is done because it is unclear whether these activities are more for work than for leisure).

Figure 4.1 shows the distribution of the total individual working hours per week for adult individuals (aged 15+), separately for men and women, as well as for urban and rural areas. Women work a much higher number of hours than men, and a larger proportion of men than women do not work at all (9.9 percent of men versus 6.4 percent of women). Similarly, individual working hours are much higher in rural than in urban areas, and the hours worked distribution in urban areas is highly skewed with a large proportion of low values. For example, while in urban areas 10.4 percent of individuals do not work any hour at all, this percentage is 6.8 in rural areas. Table 4.1 provides data on the main uses of working time (more details on the distribution of time worked are provided in appendix Tables 4.A1 and 4.A2). For example, under the first definition of working time, the mean working time in urban areas is 36.2 hours for the adult population (above 15 years of age), 38.8 hours for women, and 33.6 hours for men. While men spend more time on the labor market, the amount of time spent by women on domestic chores is much higher than for men. Girls also work longer hours than boys, again mainly due to a higher burden from domestic work, but the amount of work remains fairly reasonable, at an average of 5.5 hours per week. In rural areas by contrast, children work substantially more, for an average of 19.6 hours according to the first definition of working time. For adults, the average working time is 48.6 hours, again with a higher level for women than for men.

The average number of total working hours, the median, and the 25th and the 75th percentiles in the distribution of working hours are provided in Table 4.2 at the national level and for various groups of individuals. Clearly, throughout the distribution of time use, there are large differences between men and women, and between urban and rural areas. Using the second definition of total time worked (which includes also the time spent helping other households and in community services) slightly decreases the gender gap because men are relatively more likely than women to spend time in community services), but the qualitative results do not change. As for comparisons across urban and rural areas, the median total individual working time in rural areas is more than twice the median in

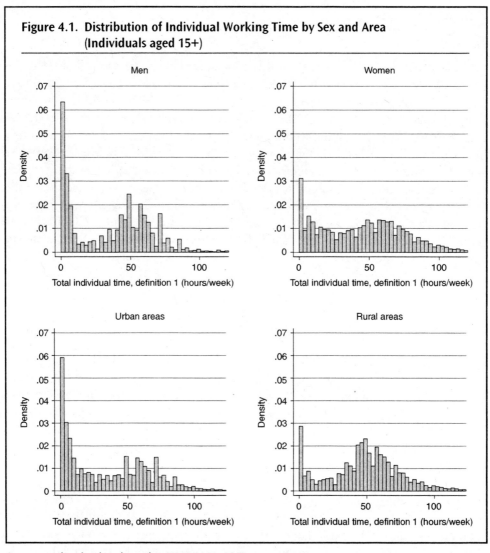

Figure 4.1. Distribution of Individual Working Time by Sex and Area (Individuals aged 15+)

Source: Authors' estimation using EIBEP 2002–2003.

urban areas. Interestingly, the gap between urban and rural areas in total individual working time according to definition 2 is larger than the gap according to definition 1 because individuals living in rural areas spend relatively more hours helping other households and in community services than urban individuals, despite their already higher total time spent in work and household activities.

Table 4.2 also provides data on time use for children. On average, children spend about 16 hours a week working in paid and unpaid tasks. The large difference between the mean and the median and the 25th and the 75th percentile suggests that these working hours are very unequally distributed. Working hours are much higher for children that do not go to school (about 25 hours/week on average) than for children that are currently in school (about 7 hours/week). Although this is not shown in the table, it is worth noting that children that

Table 4.1. Average Number of Weekly Hours Spent for Various Activities, by Sex and Age

		Age 6–14			Age 15+		
		Male	Female	All	Male	Female	All
				National level			
1	Cooking	0.2	2.3	1.2	0.2	8.5	4.8
2	Cleaning	0.4	1.6	1.0	0.4	2.6	1.6
3	Washing	0.9	1.7	1.3	0.8	2.9	1.9
4	Ironing	0.2	0.2	0.2	0.5	0.7	0.6
5	Market	0.3	0.8	0.5	0.6	2.9	1.9
6	All domestic chores (1 to 5)	1.9	6.5	4.2	2.5	17.5	10.8
7	Collection of wood	1.9	1.1	1.5	1.1	1.8	1.5
8	Collection of water	1.3	2.1	1.7	0.6	2.7	1.7
9	Aid to other households	0.2	0.3	0.2	0.8	0.8	0.8
10	Community activities	0.2	0.1	0.1	0.9	0.5	0.7
11	Work for a wage	0.4	0.5	0.5	17.8	11.6	14.4
12	Work in a farm of family business	8.0	7.8	7.9	16.9	15.8	16.3
13	Work in labor market (11 + 12)	8.4	8.3	8.4	34.7	27.4	30.7
14	**Total time (definition 1)**	13.4	18.0	15.7	38.8	49.3	44.6
15	**Total time (definition 2)**	13.8	18.4	16.1	40.5	50.6	46.1
				Urban areas			
1	Cooking	0.1	1.2	0.6	0.2	6.8	3.4
2	Cleaning	0.4	1.4	0.9	0.5	2.3	1.4
3	Washing	0.8	1.3	1.0	0.8	2.4	1.6
4	Ironing	0.2	0.2	0.2	0.7	1.1	0.9
5	Market	0.2	0.5	0.4	0.2	3.0	1.6
6	All domestic chores (1 to 5)	1.7	4.6	3.2	2.4	15.5	8.9
7	Collection of wood	0.3	0.1	0.2	0.2	0.2	0.2
8	Collection of water	0.6	0.9	0.8	0.4	1.2	0.8
9	Aid to other households	0.1	0.1	0.1	0.2	0.4	0.3
10	Community activities	0.1	0.1	0.1	0.3	0.2	0.3
11	Work for a wage	0.4	0.5	0.5	25.9	18.7	22.3
12	Work in a farm of family business	1.0	0.9	0.9	4.8	3.2	4.0
13	Work in labor market (11 + 12)	1.3	1.4	1.4	30.7	21.9	26.3
14	**Total time (definition 1)**	3.9	7.1	5.5	33.6	38.8	36.2
15	**Total time (definition 2)**	4.0	7.2	5.6	34.1	39.4	36.7
				Rural areas			
1	Cooking	0.2	2.7	1.4	0.3	9.2	5.4
2	Cleaning	0.4	1.7	1.0	0.4	2.8	1.8
3	Washing	0.9	1.8	1.3	0.7	3.1	2.1
4	Ironing	0.1	0.2	0.2	0.3	0.5	0.4

(continued)

**Table 4.1. Average Number of Weekly Hours Spent for Various Activities,
by Sex and Age (*Continued*)**

		Age 6–14			Age 15+		
		Male	Female	All	Male	Female	All
				Rural areas			
5	Market	0.3	0.8	0.6	0.9	2.8	2.0
6	All domestic chores (1 to 5)	1.9	7.3	4.5	2.6	18.3	11.7
7	Collection of wood	2.5	1.5	2.0	1.6	2.4	2.1
8	Collection of water	1.5	2.6	2.0	0.7	3.3	2.2
9	Aid to other households	0.2	0.3	0.3	1.1	1.0	1.1
10	Community activities	0.2	0.1	0.2	1.2	0.6	0.9
11	Work for a wage	0.4	0.5	0.5	13.1	8.6	10.5
12	Work in a farm of family business	10.6	10.6	10.6	23.9	21.0	22.2
13	Work in labor market (11 + 12)	11.0	11.0	11.0	37.0	29.7	32.7
14	**Total time (definition 1)**	16.9	22.4	19.6	41.8	53.7	48.7
15	**Total time (definition 2)**	17.3	22.9	20.0	44.2	55.2	50.6

Note: Zeros are included. Total time (definition 1) is the sum of 6 (all domestic chores), 7 (collection of wood), 8 (collection of water), and 13 (work in labor market). Total time (definition 2) is the sum of total time (definition 1), 9 (aid to other households), and 10 (community activities).
Source: Authors' estimation using EIBEP 2002–2003.

are out of school spend about 17 hours/week on average in *paid* work (or farm or family business), while the median of their hours of paid work is zero. The time spent in paid work by children who go to school is by contrast negligible (0.5 hours/week on average). Therefore, while almost all children who work in the labor market (or family farm or business) are out of school, the opposite is not true; moreover, a large part of child labor is spent in domestic tasks and in fetching water and wood, among children both in and out of school. Finally, as is the case for adults, girls spend more time than boys in paid and particularly unpaid work (as previous tables had suggested). The gap at the mean is 34 percent—even higher than the one existing between adult men and women (25 percent). This gap is larger for children who are enrolled in school, suggesting that it may be more difficult for girls to find the time to study, especially in rural areas.

Time Poverty

Because we have data at the individual level, we focus on individual-level measures of time poverty, although we could compute household time poverty measures as well through some aggregation procedure. In the absence of well-established practices to measure time poverty, we use two alternative relative poverty lines, a lower threshold equal to 1.5 times the median of the total individual working hours distribution and a higher threshold equal to 2 times the median. We have calculated the threshold separately for children aged 6–14

Table 4.2. Selected Values in the Cumulative Distribution of Working Time for Various Groups

	Mean	Median	25th Percentile	75th Percentile
Adult population (15 years of age and older), definition 1				
All	44.6	47.0	19.0	64.0
Men	38.8	44.0	8.0	57.0
Women	49.3	51.0	25.0	70.0
Gender gap (%)	+27.1	+15.9	+212.5	+22.8
Urban	36.2	31.0	5.0	61.0
Rural	48.7	49.0	32.0	65.0
Area gap (%)	+34.5	+58.1	+540.0	+6.6
Adult population (15 years of age and older), definition 2				
All	46.1	48.0	20.0	66.0
Men	40.5	46.0	9.0	60.0
Women	50.6	52.0	26.0	72.0
Gender gap (%)	+24.9	+13.0	+188.9	+20.0
Urban	36.7	32.0	5.0	62.0
Rural	50.6	51.0	34.0	68.0
Area gap (%)	+37.9	+59.4	+580.0	+9.7
Children (below 14 years of age), definition 1				
All	15.7	6.0	1.0	22.0
Boys	13.4	4.0	1.0	15.0
Girls	18.0	8.0	2.0	28.0
Gender gap (%)	+34.3	+100.0	+100.0	+86.7
Urban	5.5	2.0	0.0	6.0
Rural	19.6	9.0	3.0	35.0
Area gap (%)	+256.4	+350.0	n.d.	+483.3
Children (below 14 years of age), definition 1, by school enrollment status				
Not enrolled all	25.4	16.0	2.0	45.0
Not enrolled boys	24.1	13.0	1.0	45.0
Not enrolled girls	26.5	18.0	4.0	45.0
Gender gap (%)	+10.0	+38.5	+300.0	0.0
Enrolled all	6.8	4.0	1.0	9.0
Enrolled boys	5.5	3.0	0.0	7.0
Enrolled girls	8.4	5.0	1.0	11.0
Gender gap (%)	+52.7	+66.7	n.d.	+57.1

Note: Zeros are included. Total time (definition 1) is the sum of 6 (all domestic chores), 7 (collection of wood), 8 (collection of water), and 13 (work in labor market). Total time (definition 2) is the sum of total time (definition 1), 9 (aid to other households), and 10 (community activities). The "area gap" in total hours is expressed as the higher percent of total hours of rural with respect to urban area. The gender gap in total hours is expressed as the higher percent of total hours of women with respect to men, or girls with respect to boys.

Source: Authors' estimation using EIBEP 2002–2003.

Table 4.3. Time Poverty Rates (Share of individuals in the group that are time poor)

	Adult population					
	Time poverty line 70.5 hours/week			Time poverty line 94 hours/week		
	Urban	Rural	All	Urban	Rural	All
Men	11.7	8.3	9.5	2.7	1.8	2.1
Women	18.6	26.5	24.2	4.7	7.9	7.0
All	15.1	18.8	17.6	3.7	5.3	4.8
	Children					
	Time poverty line 9 hours/week			Time poverty line 12 hours/week		
	Urban	Rural	All	Urban	Rural	All
Boys	7.7	40.9	32.0	5.4	36.1	27.9
Girls	20.4	56.9	46.5	14.4	49.9	39.8
All	14.2	48.7	39.2	10.0	42.8	33.8

Note: For adults, the "time poverty line" of 70.5 hours/week corresponds to 1.5 times the median number of hours of all adults aged 15+ (47 hours/week). The "time poverty line" of 94 hours/week corresponds to 2 times the median. For children, the "time poverty line" of 9 hours/week corresponds to 1.5 times the median number of hours of work among children and the "time poverty line" of 12 hours/week corresponds to 2 times the median among children.
Source: Authors' estimation using EIBEP 2002–2003.

and adults aged based on their own respective distribution. The resulting poverty lines are 9 hours and 70.5 hours per week for the lower threshold for children and adults respectively, and 12 hours and 94 hours for the higher threshold.

Table 4.3 shows the time poverty rates based on the two alternative poverty lines for men and women living in urban and rural areas. According to the lower threshold about 18 percent of all individuals are time poor. This rate is much higher for women (24.2 percent) than men (9.5 percent), and in rural areas (18.8 percent) as compared to urban areas (15.1 percent). More women living in rural areas are time poor (26.5 percent) than women living in urban area (18.6 percent). For men, it is the reverse, with urban men more likely to be time poor than rural men (11.7 vs. 8.3 percent). When we adopt a higher threshold the time poverty rates are lower, with he overall time poverty rate dropping to 4.8 percent, but the patterns in terms of comparisons between groups are very similar. The differences between men and women are in this case even larger—moving from the lower to the higher threshold makes time poverty rates for women decrease by a factor of 3, while time poverty rates for men decrease by a factor of almost 5.

Table 4.3 also shows the child time poverty rates. Given that the time poverty lines have been computed separately for children and adults, in each case with reference to *their own* hour distribution, we may very well have higher relative rates of time poverty among children than among adults since both the lower and the higher time poverty lines turn out to be significantly lower than for adults, at 9 and 12 hours/week respectively. Looking first at the results obtained with the lower threshold, we notice that the time poverty rates are again much higher in rural (49 percent) than in urban areas (14 percent); they are also

Table 4.4. Time Poverty Gap and Squared Time Poverty Gap

| | Time poverty gap, adult population | | | | | |
| | Time poverty line 70.5 hours/week | | | Time poverty line 94 hours/week | | |
	Urban	Rural	All	Urban	Rural	All
Men	2.8	1.9	2.2	0.6	0.4	0.5
Women	4.4	7.1	6.3	0.7	1.4	1.2
All	3.6	4.9	4.5	0.7	1.0	0.9
	Squared time poverty gap, adult population					
	Time poverty line 70.5 hours/week			Time poverty line 94 hours/week		
	Urban	Rural	All	Urban	Rural	All
Men	1.4	0.9	1.1	0.2	0.1	0.2
Women	1.9	3.3	2.9	0.2	0.4	0.3
All	1.6	2.3	2.1	0.2	0.3	0.3

Note: For adults, the "time poverty line" of 70.5 hours/week corresponds to 1.5 times the median number of hours of all adults aged 15+ (47 hours/week). The "time poverty line" of 94 hours/week corresponds to 2 times the median.
Source: Authors' estimation using EIBEP 2002–2003.

higher for girls (47 percent) than for boys (32 percent). Using the higher threshold decreases the time poverty rates somewhat, but the same pattern arises.

In order to illustrate the use of higher poverty measures, we provide time poverty gap and squared time poverty gaps for the adult population in Table 4.4, using the time poverty line for the normalization. As for Table 4.3, all values have been multiplied by 100. The key conclusions in terms of comparing urban and rural areas, as well as men and women, are the same with these measures as what was observed with the headcount index.

Correlates of Time Poverty

What are the determinants or correlates of time poverty? To answer this question we ran probit regressions to explain the probability of being time poor as a function of personal, household and area variables. The analysis is again carried out at the individual level, that is, each individual is classified as time poor or not depending on his or her own individual total time worked. Among the regressors we included, beside the usual demographic variables (age, sex, and marital status), the educational qualifications, religion, the consumption quintile of the household, the number of infants (aged 0–5) and children (aged 6–14), adults (aged 15–64) and senior people (aged over 65), and their square values. We also included dummy variables for the presence of disabled people, and for households with only women.[12] Finally, we included geographical dummies for rural/urban areas and for the region of residence. Separate regressions were estimated for men and women, as well as for rural and urban areas. The results are reported in Table 4.5.

---

12. We preferred this variable to the alternative "female headed household," because many female headed households include several adult men.

Table 4.5. Probit Regression for the Probability of Being Time Poor
(Lower time poverty line)

	All	Men	Women	Men Urban	Men Rural	Women Urban	Women Rural
Age	0.012***	0.010***	0.015***	0.015***	0.003**	0.019***	0.012***
	(0.001)	(0.001)	(0.001)	(0.001)	(0.001)	(0.002)	(0.002)
Age squared	−0.000***	−0.000***	−0.000***	−0.000***	−0.000***	−0.000***	−0.000***
	(0.000)	(0.000)	(0.000)	(0.000)	(0.000)	(0.000)	(0.000)
Female	0.033***						
	(0.006)						
Rural	−0.067***	−0.037***	0.014*				
	(0.007)	(0.006)	(0.008)				
Female*rural	0.101***						
	(0.010)						
Disabled	−0.087***	−0.045***	−0.139***	−0.043***	−0.044***	−0.122***	−0.159***
	(0.007)	(0.009)	(0.011)	(0.013)	(0.012)	(0.013)	(0.018)
Monogamous	0.077***	0.015*	0.138***	0.021*	−0.001	0.108***	0.130***
	(0.008)	(0.009)	(0.014)	(0.011)	(0.013)	(0.016)	(0.024)
Poligamous	0.079***	0.013	0.132***	0.023	0.005	0.100***	0.126***
	(0.009)	(0.011)	(0.014)	(0.016)	(0.015)	(0.018)	(0.022)
Divorced	0.088***	0.051*	0.140***	0.029	0.071	0.106***	0.128***
	(0.019)	(0.028)	(0.027)	(0.034)	(0.044)	(0.031)	(0.045)
Widow/er	0.023*	0.030	0.070***	0.029	0.022	0.066**	0.028
	(0.014)	(0.036)	(0.021)	(0.052)	(0.044)	(0.026)	(0.032)
Christian	0.023***	0.002	0.049***	−0.010	0.025	0.006	0.187***
	(0.009)	(0.009)	(0.014)	(0.011)	(0.018)	(0.015)	(0.030)
Other religion	0.008	0.009	0.014	0.130**	0.009	−0.074*	0.175***
	(0.013)	(0.016)	(0.020)	(0.065)	(0.019)	(0.040)	(0.035)
Primary	−0.068***	−0.049***	−0.078***	−0.048***	−0.043***	−0.055***	−0.142***
	(0.005)	(0.005)	(0.010)	(0.006)	(0.008)	(0.011)	(0.023)
Secondary 1st	−0.077***	−0.054***	−0.095***	−0.058***	−0.029*	−0.083***	0.026
	(0.006)	(0.005)	(0.012)	(0.006)	(0.017)	(0.011)	(0.119)
Secondary 2nd	−0.078***	−0.050***	−0.122***	−0.056***	0.008	−0.097***	
	(0.014)	(0.010)	(0.036)	(0.010)	(0.084)	(0.035)	
Technical	−0.078***	−0.050***	−0.108***	−0.065***	0.086	−0.095***	
	(0.008)	(0.007)	(0.016)	(0.007)	(0.056)	(0.014)	
University	−0.093***	−0.065***	−0.089***	−0.073***	−0.048*	−0.086***	
	(0.007)	(0.005)	(0.033)	(0.005)	(0.027)	(0.026)	
Unknown ed.	−0.013	−0.047*	0.021	−0.041		−0.045	0.140
	(0.033)	(0.029)	(0.054)	(0.037)		(0.051)	(0.107)

(continued)

Table 4.5. Probit Regression for the Probability of Being Time Poor
            (Lower time poverty line) (*Continued*)

	All	Men	Women	Men Urban	Men Rural	Women Urban	Women Rural
Infants (0–5)	−0.003	0.005	−0.010**	0.006	0.010**	−0.010	−0.009
	(0.003)	(0.003)	(0.004)	(0.006)	(0.004)	(0.007)	(0.006)
Infants squared	0.001**	0.000	0.001**	−0.001	−0.000	0.001	0.001*
	(0.000)	(0.000)	(0.001)	(0.001)	(0.001)	(0.001)	(0.001)
Children (6–14)	−0.005**	−0.007***	−0.003	−0.012***	−0.001	0.001	−0.004
	(0.002)	(0.002)	(0.003)	(0.003)	(0.003)	(0.004)	(0.005)
Children squared	0.001***	0.000**	0.001***	0.001**	0.000	0.000	0.001***
	(0.000)	(0.000)	(0.000)	(0.000)	(0.000)	(0.000)	(0.000)
Adults (15–64)	−0.013***	−0.003*	−0.025***	−0.000	−0.015***	−0.020***	−0.041***
	(0.001)	(0.002)	(0.002)	(0.002)	(0.005)	(0.003)	(0.007)
Adults squared	0.000***	0.000	0.001***	−0.000	0.001**	0.001***	0.001**
	(0.000)	(0.000)	(0.000)	(0.000)	(0.000)	(0.000)	(0.001)
Seniors (65+)	0.011	0.005	0.012	0.015	−0.005	0.013	0.005
	(0.007)	(0.009)	(0.011)	(0.012)	(0.012)	(0.015)	(0.018)
Seniors squared	−0.007*	−0.002	−0.010*	−0.005	−0.002	−0.003	−0.017*
	(0.004)	(0.005)	(0.006)	(0.006)	(0.006)	(0.007)	(0.009)
Disabled ind.	0.003	−0.007	0.012	−0.019**	0.013	−0.005	0.029**
	(0.005)	(0.006)	(0.009)	(0.008)	(0.010)	(0.011)	(0.014)
Only women	0.021*		0.015			0.021	−0.003
	(0.012)		(0.015)			(0.022)	(0.021)
2nd quintile	0.011	0.026**	−0.000	0.023	0.029**	0.015	−0.015
	(0.008)	(0.011)	(0.011)	(0.020)	(0.012)	(0.021)	(0.014)
3rd quintile	0.027***	0.026**	0.031***	0.027	0.021	0.015	0.043***
	(0.008)	(0.010)	(0.012)	(0.018)	(0.013)	(0.020)	(0.016)
4th quintile	0.025***	0.037***	0.016	0.027	0.056***	0.012	0.013
	(0.008)	(0.011)	(0.012)	(0.018)	(0.015)	(0.019)	(0.017)
5th quintile	0.036***	0.044***	0.032***	0.037**	0.057***	0.028	0.029
	(0.008)	(0.011)	(0.012)	(0.018)	(0.017)	(0.020)	(0.018)
Conakry	−0.005	0.032***	−0.046***	0.032***		−0.005	
	(0.008)	(0.010)	(0.011)	(0.011)		(0.014)	
Faranah	0.010	0.001	0.015	0.018	−0.022*	0.057***	−0.036**
	(0.008)	(0.010)	(0.013)	(0.015)	(0.013)	(0.019)	(0.018)
Kankan	−0.005	0.028**	−0.032***	0.003	0.048***	0.016	−0.077***
	(0.008)	(0.011)	(0.011)	(0.014)	(0.017)	(0.018)	(0.015)
Kindia	0.022***	0.021*	0.023*	0.019	0.023	0.055***	−0.010
	(0.008)	(0.011)	(0.013)	(0.015)	(0.015)	(0.019)	(0.018)

(*continued*)

Table 4.5. Probit Regression for the Probability of Being Time Poor (Lower time poverty line) (*Continued*)

	All	Men	Women	Men Urban	Men Rural	Women Urban	Women Rural
Labe	−0.021***	0.018	−0.054***	0.006	0.032*	−0.002	−0.106***
	(0.008)	(0.012)	(0.011)	(0.015)	(0.019)	(0.018)	(0.015)
Mamou	0.034***	0.037***	0.031**	0.064***	−0.004	0.050**	0.008
	(0.010)	(0.014)	(0.014)	(0.020)	(0.016)	(0.021)	(0.020)
Nzerekore	−0.044***	0.011	−0.094***	0.010	−0.000	0.008	−0.230***
	(0.007)	(0.011)	(0.010)	(0.014)	(0.016)	(0.017)	(0.014)
Observed probability	0.161	0.096	0.217	0.106	0.082	0.185	0.255
Predicted probability	0.130	0.081	0.183	0.084	0.069	0.154	0.215
Pseudo R²	0.110	0.066	0.103	0.091	0.056	0.101	0.115
Log likelihood	−11711	−4074	−7527	−2583	−1424	−3747	−3681
Number of observations	29793	13761	16032	8419	5334	8699	7325

Notes: Marginal effects (rather than coefficients) shown in the table. The marginal effect is computed at the mean of regressors. For dummy variables it is given for a discrete change from 0 to 1. Standard errors in parentheses; *significant at 10%; **significant at 5%; ***significant at 1%. Sample is restricted to individuals aged 15+. "Adults" are individuals aged 15–64; "seniors" are individuals aged 65+. The 'time poverty line' is 70.5 hours/week. The reference categories are: male, not disabled, urban, single never married, muslin, no education level (or never in school), no children aged 0–5 in the household, no children aged 6–14 in the household, no disabled people in the household, household with also men, first consumption quintile, and living in Boke. Predicted probability computed at the mean of the regressors.
Source: Authors' estimation using EIBEP 2002–2003.

Table 4.5 gives the marginal effects estimated at the mean of the variables rather than the coefficients—for dummy variables the marginal effect represents the change in probability when the dummy variable changes from 0 to 1. For example, the first column (pooled regression) indicates that women are 3 percentage points more likely to be time poor than men; for women living in rural area this probability increases by an additional 10 percentage points. The coefficient of living in rural areas is estimated to be negative (−7 percentage points), but this is driven by the male sample; by comparing the marginal effect of the rural dummy reported in columns 2 and 3, where different regressions are estimated for men and women, we notice that men living in rural area are *less* likely to be time poor, while for women the opposite is true. Obviously, being disabled significantly and substantially decreases the probability of being time poor, given that disabled people are less able to work in paid and unpaid tasks. Marital status is also associated with variations in the probability of being time poor, but this effect is significant (and substantial) only for women. Married women (either in monogamous or polygamous union) are more likely to be time poor than single never married women (about 10–11 percentage points more in urban area and 13 percentage points in rural area; see columns 6 and 7). A similar effect is estimated for divorced women. Interestingly, women living in rural areas who are Christian or belong to a religion other than Muslim are more likely to be time poor, about 18–19 percentage points more than Muslim rural women.

The educational qualification is also a powerful predictor of time poverty, for both men and women, and especially in urban areas. Increasing education is associated with lower probabilities of being time poor; in rural areas where people with qualifications above primary education are extremely rare, especially among women, having completed primary education makes individual less likely to be time poor compared to those with no educational qualifications (–4 percentage points for men and –14 percentage points for women). By contrast, well-being measured by the consumption quintile appears to be more weakly associated with time poverty. A significant effect exists for men living in rural area—those in the top 4th and 5th quintile are about 6 percentage points more likely to be time poor than the poorer men. For men living in urban areas, those in the 5th quintile are 4 percentage points more likely to be time poor. However, no significant effect is estimated for women (except that women living in rural area who are in the 3rd quintile are 4 percentage points more likely to be time poor than the remaining women).

The coefficients for the number of infants and children do not provide a clear story. We included these variables among the regressors to test the idea that the presence of young children may require more time from adult members (but recall that time spent in childcare is not explicitly collected in the survey), while older children may provide substitute labor and therefore make adult members save time. In fact, a positive coefficient is estimated only for men living in rural areas—indicating that only for this group each extra child increases the probability of being time poor (1 percentage point for each additional child). On the other hand, a negative coefficient for the number of older children is estimated for men living in urban areas—for them each extra child aged 6–14 decreases the probability of being time poor, at a decreasing rate (so that one child decreases this probability by 1 percent, while at six children the change in probability is zero and after that the variation becomes slightly positive). Women's time poverty, by contrast, does not seem to be affected by the number of either young or older children living in the household. More adults in the household, on the other hand, make everybody less likely to be time poor, indicating that the workload will be more equally distributed across members. This effect is stronger for women living in rural area (the first adult decreases the time poverty probability by about 4 percentage points, and each subsequent adult slightly less than that); smaller marginal effects are estimated for women living in urban area and men living in rural area. The presence of disabled people in the household increase the probability of being time poor for women living in rural areas (about 3 percentage points), while it decreases the probability of being time poor for men living in urban areas by about 2 percentage points. Finally, there are also geographical differences in the probability of being time poor according to Guinea's main natural regions.

Conclusion

Time poverty has long been recognized as a constraint to development in Sub-Saharan Africa, with women working especially long hours due in part to a lack of access to basic infrastructure services such as water and electricity, but also due to the rising demands from the "care economy." The very concept of time poverty and the evidence on high workloads for women could be of use for policymakers. However, when combined with other dimensions of welfare, such as consumption or income poverty, the analysis of time poverty can be even more revealing. Other papers in this volume provide simulations of the impact that increases in hours of work (working up to a certain time poverty line or norm) could have on monetary poverty. The gains from what could be referred to as full employment can be compared to gains that would be achieved from higher pay per hour working.

Apart from looking at the link between time poverty and consumption or income poverty, work also needs to be carried out on the relationship between time poverty and other development outcomes. When looking at the targets set out in the Millennium Development Goals, it is clear that the time spent by children working may have a detrimental impact on their enrollment in school. Yet, time poverty may also affect other outcomes, such as the nutritional status of children. Conversely, conditions related to health (such as the HIV/AIDS crisis) may increase time poverty and thereby reduce the amount of time that households and individuals may allocate to work.

Despite a growing number of studies on time use in Africa and elsewhere, time poverty has remained loosely defined. In this paper, we have argued that the techniques used for the measurement and analysis of the determinants of poverty can be applied readily to the issue of time poverty. While the concepts and examples presented in this paper have not dealt with the issue of the impact of time poverty on development outcomes, we hope that they have provided some ideas on how to use the measurement and analysis techniques that have been developed for the analysis of monetary poverty in this new and exciting area of work that time poverty represents.

References

Apps, P. 2004. "Gender, Time Use, and Models of the Household." Policy Research Working Paper Series: 3233, The World Bank, Washington, D.C.

Apps, P., and R. Rees. 2004. "The Household, Time Use and Tax Policy." *CESifo Economic Studies* 50:479–500.

Blackden, C.M., and C. Bhanu. 1999. *Gender, Growth, and Poverty Reduction*. Special Program of Assistance for Africa 1998 Status Report on Poverty, World Bank Technical Paper No. 428, Washington, D.C.

Charmes, J. 2005. "A Review of Empirical Evidence on Time Use in Africa from UN-sponsored Surveys." (Chapter 3 of this volume.)

Coudouel, A., J. Hentschel, and Q. Wodon. 2002. "Poverty Measurement and Analysis." In J. Klugman, editor, *A Sourcebook for Poverty Reduction Strategies, Volume 1: Core Techniques and Cross-Cutting Issues*. Washington, D.C.: The World Bank.

Foster, J.E., J. Greer, and E. Thorbecke. 1984. "A Class of Decomposable Poverty Indices." *Econometrica* 52:761–766.

Gelb, A. 2001. "Gender and Growth: Africa's Missed Potential." Findings No. 197, Africa Region, The World Bank, Washington, D.C.

Hamermesh, D.S., and G.A. Pfann, eds. 2005. *The Economics of Time Use*. Contributions to Economic Analysis, vol. 271. Amsterdam, San Diego and Oxford: Elsevier.

Hamermesh, D.S., H. Frazis, and J. Stewart. 2005. "Data Watch: The American Time Use Survey." *Journal of Economic Perspectives* 19:221–32.

Harvey, A.S., and M.E. Taylor. 2004. "Time Use." In M. Grosh and P. Glewwe, eds., *Designing Household Survey Questionaires: Lessons from Fifteen Years of the Living Standards Measurement Study*. Washington, D.C.: The World Bank.

Ilahi, N. 2000. "The Intra-household Allocation of Time and Tasks: What Have We Learnt from the Empirical Literature?" Policy Research Report on Gender and Development, Working Paper Series No. 13, World Bank Development Research Group, Washington, D.C.

Ilahi, N. 2001. "Gender and the Allocation of Adult Time: Evidence from the Peru LSMS Panel Data." Policy Research Working Paper Series No. 2744, The World Bank, Washington, D.C.

Ilahi, N., and F. Grimard. 2001. "Public Infrastructure and Private Costs: Water Supply and Time Allocation of Women in Rural Pakistan." *Economic Development and Cultural Change* 49:45–75.

Makdissi, P., and Q. Wodon. 2004. "Robust Comparisons of Natural Resource Depletion Indices." *Economics Bulletin* 9(2):1–9.

Newman, C. 2002. "Gender, Time Use, and Change: The Impact of the Cut Flower Industry in Ecuador." *World Bank Economic Review* 16: 375–95.

Zhang, J., H. Timmermans, and A. Borgers. 2005. "A Model of Household Task Allocation and Time Use." *Transportation Research: Part B: Methodological* 39:81–95.

Vickery, C. 1977. "The Time-Poor: A New Look at Poverty." *Journal of Human Resources* 12:27–48.

Wodon, Q., and K. Beegle. 2005. "Labor Shortages Despite Underemployment? Seasonality in Time Use in Malawi." (Chapter 5 in this volume.)

World Bank. 2001. *Engendering Development: Through Gender Equality in Rights, Resources, and Voice*. World Bank Policy Research Report. Washington, D.C.

Appendix Table 4A.1. Number of Weekly Hours Spent for Various Activities, by Sex, Time Spent Collecting Water, and Urban/Rural Area

		Men 15+				Women 15+			
Urban		0 Hrs	1–4 Hrs	4+ Hrs	All	0 Hrs	1–4 Hrs	4+ Hrs	All
1	Cooking	0.1	0.5	0.4	0.2	5.6	7.8	10.8	6.8
2	Cleaning	0.3	1.2	2.3	0.5	1.8	2.6	4.5	2.3
3	Washing	0.6	1.7	3.7	0.8	1.8	2.8	4.6	2.4
4	Ironing	0.5	1.3	2.6	0.7	0.8	1.3	2.1	1.1
5	Market	0.1	0.4	0.7	0.2	2.4	3.4	5.9	3.0
6	**All domestic chores (1–5)**	**1.6**	**5.1**	**9.6**	**2.4**	**12.5**	**17.8**	**27.7**	**15.5**
7	Collection of wood	0.1	0.4	0.8	0.2	0.1	0.3	0.4	0.2
8	Collection of water	0.0	1.6	7.5	0.4	0.0	1.9	7.5	1.2
9	Aid to other households	0.2	0.4	0.3	0.2	0.2	0.5	0.9	0.4
10	Community activities	0.3	0.3	0.2	0.3	0.2	0.3	0.4	0.2
11	Work for a wage	28.3	16.9	8.7	25.9	18.4	18.9	20.4	18.7
12	Work in a farm of family business	4.7	5.1	6.0	4.8	2.6	4.0	3.9	3.2
13	**Work in labor market (1 + 12)**	**33.0**	**21.9**	**14.8**	**30.7**	**21.0**	**22.9**	**24.3**	**21.9**
14	**Total time (definition 1)**	**34.7**	**29.0**	**32.6**	**33.6**	**33.5**	**42.9**	**60.0**	**38.8**
15	**Total time (definition 2)**	**35.2**	**29.7**	**33.1**	**34.1**	**33.9**	**43.7**	**61.3**	**39.4**
Rural									
1	Cooking	0.1	0.8	1.4	0.3	4.8	9.4	13.2	9.2
2	Cleaning	0.2	0.9	1.3	0.4	1.3	2.4	4.9	2.8
3	Washing	0.3	1.5	4.2	0.7	1.3	2.8	5.5	3.1
4	Ironing	0.2	0.8	0.8	0.3	0.2	0.5	0.7	0.5
5	Market	0.8	0.9	2.2	0.9	1.3	2.7	4.5	2.8
6	**All domestic chores (1–5)**	**1.6**	**4.9**	**9.9**	**2.6**	**8.9**	**17.9**	**28.9**	**18.3**
7	Collection of wood	1.2	2.4	7.1	1.6	0.9	2.1	4.6	2.4
8	Collection of water	0.0	1.7	8.8	0.7	0.0	2.2	9.0	3.3
9	Aid to other households	1.1	1.1	1.3	1.1	0.5	1.0	1.5	1.0
10	Community activities	1.3	0.9	1.1	1.2	0.3	0.6	0.8	0.6
11	Work for a wage	13.4	12.3	10.8	13.1	6.5	8.9	10.2	8.6
12	Work in a farm of family business	25.1	20.1	21.8	23.9	15.8	22.6	23.2	21.0
13	**Work in labor market (11 + 12)**	**38.5**	**32.4**	**32.6**	**37.0**	**22.3**	**31.5**	**33.4**	**29.7**
14	**Total time (definition 1)**	**41.2**	**41.4**	**58.4**	**41.8**	**32.1**	**53.6**	**75.9**	**53.7**
15	**Total time (definition 2)**	**43.7**	**43.4**	**60.8**	**44.2**	**32.9**	**55.2**	**78.2**	**55.2**

Note: Zeros are included. Total time (definition 1) is the sum of 6 (all domestic chores), 7 (collection of wood), 8 (collection of water), and 13 (work in labor market). Total time (definition 2) is the sum of total time (definition 1), 9 (aid to other households), and 10 (community activities).

Source: Authors' estimation using EIBEP 2002–2003.

Appendix Table 4A.2. Number of Weekly Hours Spent for Various Activities, by Sex, Time Spent Collecting Wood, and Urban/Rural Area

		Men 15+				Women 15+			
Urban		0 Hrs	1–4 Hrs	4+ Hrs	All	0 Hrs	1–4 Hrs	4+ Hrs	All
1	Cooking	0.1	0.7	0.3	0.2	6.7	7.5	11.7	6.8
2	Cleaning	0.5	0.9	1.3	0.5	2.2	2.5	5.0	2.3
3	Washing	0.8	1.2	1.9	0.8	2.3	2.5	5.5	2.4
4	Ironing	0.6	1.0	1.5	0.7	1.0	1.3	2.6	1.1
5	Market	0.2	0.7	0.2	0.2	3.0	2.9	6.0	3.0
6	**All domestic chores (1–5)**	**2.2**	**4.6**	**5.2**	**2.4**	**15.3**	**16.8**	**30.7**	**15.5**
7	Collection of wood	0.0	1.6	9.1	0.2	0.0	1.6	8.0	0.2
8	Collection of water	0.3	1.0	1.6	0.4	1.1	1.9	3.1	1.2
9	Aid to other households	0.2	0.7	1.1	0.2	0.3	0.7	1.3	0.4
10	Community activities	0.3	0.7	1.1	0.3	0.2	0.7	1.4	0.2
11	Work for a wage	26.3	20.2	12.5	25.9	18.6	20.0	22.6	18.7
12	Work in a farm of family business	4.7	4.9	15.7	4.8	3.1	3.7	8.1	3.2
13	**Work in labor market (11 + 12)**	**31.0**	**25.1**	**28.2**	**30.7**	**21.7**	**23.7**	**30.7**	**21.9**
14	**Total time (definition 1)**	**33.6**	**32.2**	**44.1**	**33.6**	**38.1**	**43.9**	**72.4**	**38.8**
15	**Total time (definition 2)**	**34.1**	**33.6**	**46.2**	**34.1**	**38.6**	**45.3**	**75.1**	**39.4**
Rural									
1	Cooking	0.1	0.5	0.5	0.3	7.1	9.2	13.9	9.2
2	Cleaning	0.2	0.6	0.8	0.4	2.2	2.6	4.7	2.8
3	Washing	0.2	1.1	2.2	0.7	2.1	2.9	6.1	3.1
4	Ironing	0.1	0.5	0.6	0.3	0.2	0.6	0.9	0.5
5	Market	0.7	1.0	1.6	0.9	2.0	2.6	5.0	2.8
6	**All domestic chores (1–5)**	**1.3**	**3.7**	**5.6**	**2.6**	**13.6**	**17.9**	**30.5**	**18.3**
7	Collection of wood	0.0	2.1	8.8	1.6	0.0	2.3	8.4	2.4
8	Collection of water	0.2	0.9	2.4	0.7	2.0	3.1	7.0	3.3
9	Aid to other households	1.0	1.2	1.4	1.1	0.6	1.1	1.7	1.0
10	Community activities	1.2	1.1	1.6	1.2	0.3	0.7	0.9	0.6
11	Work for a wage	14.8	11.3	10.2	13.1	6.6	9.0	12.1	8.6
12	Work in a farm of family business	23.0	24.4	26.7	23.9	18.6	22.3	23.0	21.0
13	**Work in labor market (11 + 12)**	**37.8**	**35.7**	**36.9**	**37.0**	**25.2**	**31.3**	**35.1**	**29.7**
14	**Total time (definition 1)**	**39.2**	**42.4**	**53.7**	**41.8**	**40.8**	**54.4**	**81.0**	**53.7**
15	**Total time (definition 2)**	**41.4**	**44.7**	**56.7**	**44.2**	**41.7**	**56.2**	**83.7**	**55.2**

Note: Zeros are included. Total time (definition 1) is the sum of 6 (all domestic chores), 7 (collection of wood), 8 (collection of water), and 13 (work in labor market). Total time (definition 2) is the sum of total time (definition 1), 9 (aid to other households), and 10 (community activities).

Source: Authors' estimation using EIBEP 2002–2003.

CHAPTER 5

Labor Shortages Despite Underemployment? Seasonality in Time Use in Malawi

Quentin Wodon and Kathleen Beegle[13]

Evidence for Malawi and other developing countries suggests the existence of labor shortages at the peak of the cropping season, with negative impacts on the ability of households to make the most of their endowments such as land. At the same time, for most of the year, there is substantial underemployment, especially in rural areas. It could therefore be argued that seasonality in the demand for labor is leading to both underemployment and labor shortages. This paper provides basic descriptive data from a 2004 nationally representative household survey to assess the typical workload of the population. The data confirm the presence of strong seasonality effects in the supply of labor, as well as substantial differences in workload between men and women due to the burden of domestic work, including the time spent for collecting water and wood.

The issue of seasonality in labor demand and supply in developing countries has been discussed extensively in the literature. For example, using household panel data from India, Skoufias (1993, 1994) suggests the presence of significant intertemporal substitution in the labor supply of women, but not of men. Dercon and Krishnan (2000) use data from rural Ethiopia to show high levels of seasonal and year-to-year variability in consumption and poverty, with households also responding to changes in labor demand and prices. Pitt and Khandker (2002) show how group-based credit mechanisms used to fund self-employment by landless households in Bangladesh help to smooth

13. The authors are with the World Bank. This work was prepared as a contribution to the Poverty Assessment for Malawi prepared at the World Bank. The authors acknowledge support from the GENFUND as well as the Belgian Poverty Reduction Partnership for research on this issue as part of a small research program on gender, time use and poverty in Sub-Saharan Africa. Preliminary results from the paper were presented at a World Bank workshop on the topic in November 2005. The views expressed here are those of the authors and need not reflect those of the World Bank, its Executive Directors or the countries they represent.

seasonal patterns of consumption and even out male labor supply. Ellis (2000) suggests that households adopt multiple livelihood strategies in part to deal with seasonality, with diversified rural livelihoods leading to a reduction in vulnerability. Finally, using data from India, Kanwar (2004) analyzes how labor supply and demand respond to wages in the agricultural market for daily-rated labor. While the agricultural labor market is in equilibrium during the rainy season, it experiences excess supply in the post-rainy season.

The importance of seasonality in the allocation of rural farm labor in Malawi is also relatively well documented. For example, Kamanga (2002) provides seasonal cropping and labor calendars for two villages. The first village, Chisepo, is located in the Kasungu area. The village has a semi-arid to sub-humid climate with unimodal rainfall from November to April (the annual rainfall is estimated at 845 mm with a mean temperature of 25°C). Farmers cultivate tobacco, maize and groundnut on soils of low to moderate fertility. The second village is Songani, in the Zomba area. Rainfalls are concentrated between October and April, with *Chiperoni* rains from May to July. The total annual rainfalls vary from 800 to 1,200 mm, and the mean temperature is 22.5°C. Apart from maize, farmers also cultivate cassava, pigeon peas, groundnuts, beans, and pumpkins. Farming is seasonally driven, with few differences between the two villages. In both villages the periods of highest intensity of labor are concentrated in December–January, as shown in Tables 5.1 and 5.2 where the dark shaded areas represent high labor intensity.

As explained by Brummett (2002), the fact that labor is scarce at some periods of the year has implications for the ability of farmers to diversify and enter into new activities. In the case of aquaculture, apart from the seasonal availability of inputs for the ponds, the availability of water and labor are constraining aquaculture adoption and production. That is, household labor is required for the production of staple crops precisely when inputs for aquaculture are available. Brummett argues that such constraints to the development of aquaculture are seldom recognized in analytical work and programs.

A large sample study for Malawi by Tango International (2003) based on a household survey conducted in 2003–2004 with data on 2030 households identified the scarcity of labor as an important constraint to the development of rural farming. The most common reason cited by households for not cultivating all of their land was a lack of inputs such as fertilizer and pesticides (cited by 62.7 percent of households). This was followed by the lack of labor (44.5 percent), and the lack of seeds (21.1 percent). Other reasons cited for not cultivating all the land available were the lack of rainfall (5 percent), the need to leave land as fallow in order to conserve soil fertility (2.6 percent), and other reasons (13.5 percent). When combined with an analysis of the level of vulnerability of the households in the sample, it appeared that more vulnerable households were more likely to cite the lack of labor as the main constraint to farming all their available land.

Another interesting finding from the Tango International study relates to the relationship between labor availability and food security. Households were asked why their food stock expectations had decreased for the current harvest as compared to a normal harvest, which led to a lack of food for many. Most households associated the insufficient availability of food to a lack of inputs, an issue likely to be related to the recent reduction in input subsidies provided by the government (Starter Packs which contain, among other items, fertilizer). The impacts of droughts and "other reasons" came in as the second and third most important reasons for a lack of sufficient food. The lack of labor ranked fourth, before the lack of land, poor soils, not enough seeds, and draught power. There are signs

Table 5.1. Seasonality in Cropping Activities, Kasungu, Northern Malawi

Crops	June	July	August	September	October	November	December	January	February	March	April	May
Maize	Harvesting		Clearing and ridging	Planting *dimba* clearing and ridging		Planting, weeding, and fertilizing (1)		Fertilizing (2) and weeding (2)	Weeding (2) and bunding			Harvesting
Groundnuts	Harvesting and clearing											
Tobacco			Nursery activities			Planting		Weeding	Picking, processing, and uprooting stems			Clearing
Sweet Potatoes	Harvesting					Planting, fertilizing (1) and (2), weeding (1), and bunding						
Chickpeas						Planting		Planting			Harvesting	
Beans						Planting			Harvesting			

Note: Dark shaded areas represent high labor intensity.

Source: Kamanga (2002).

Table 5.2. Seasonality in Cropping Activities, Zomba, Southern Malawi

Crops	June	July	August	September	October	November	December	January	February	March	April	May
Maize	Incorporation of residues (clearing)		Incorporation of residues and ridging		Ridging, planting, weeding (1) and fertilizing (1)			Weeding (2) and fertilizing (2)	Weedubg (2) and bunding	Harvesting		Harvesting
Groundnut						Planting		Weeding				Harvesting
Pigeons peas	Harvesting and clearing					Planting and weeding		Weeding			Harvesting	
Cassava		Planting and ridging										
Sweet potatoes	Harvesting											
Mucuna						Planting at low population densities		Planting				
Chick peas						Planting					Harvesting	
Beans						Planting					Harvesting	

Note: Dark shaded areas represent high labor intensity.
Source: Kamanga (2002).

that the problem of a lack of labor is being exacerbated by the HIV/AIDS crisis. Apart from the direct impact of death itself, caring for the sick, and burying the dead has led to a reduction in the time available for productive activities (Shah and others 2001).[14]

The above evidence for Malawi on labor shortages suggests that such shortages are temporary, but that they do have a negative effect on the ability of households to make the most of their endowments. It could be argued that seasonality in the demand for labor is leading to both underemployment and labor shortages. For most of the year, household members have extra time available to undertake productive ventures, but many do not because of the limited opportunities available to them. At the peak of the cropping season, around December–January, the demands in the agriculture sector make it difficult to find the labor necessary to perform all the work that has to be done. In addition, time constraints may force household to conduct necessary tasks (such as planting and weeding) at suboptimal times, thereby reducing yields.

The contribution of this paper is to provide basic yet detailed statistics from recent household survey data on time use patterns in Malawi. This is done using a 2004 nationally representative household survey that includes questions on time use. Because the survey was implemented over a 13-month period, we can analyze changes in the patterns of time use between households who were interviewed at different periods of the year. We limit the analysis to providing basic statistics on the allocation of time by individuals to different tasks at different periods of the year, with breakdowns according to age, gender, and the status of the household in the distribution of consumption per capita. The results in the next section confirm the presence of strong seasonality in time use. The brief conclusion that follows suggests that seasonality leads to different policy implications as compared to a situation without such seasonality.

Data and Empirical Results

This paper provides measures of time use in Malawi using the 2004 Second Integrated Household Survey. Data are available for all household members in the sample of 11,280 households (a total of over 52,000 individuals). The questions on time use are asked to all individuals above 4 years of age. More specifically, the employment and time use model in the survey asks the following questions to all household members above 4 years of age:

(a) How many hours did you spend yesterday cooking, doing laundry, cleaning your house, and the like?
(b) How many hours did you spend yesterday collecting firewood (or other fuel materials)?
(c) How many hours in the last seven days did you spend on household agricultural activities (including livestock) or fishing, whether for sale or for household food?

---

14. In contrast, in labor surplus areas, on average there may be no observable impact of a prime-age death on the labor supply of surviving household members, as suggested in a study of northwest Tanzania by Beegle (2005).

(d) How many hours in the last seven days did you do any work for a wage, salary, commission, or any payment in kind, excluding *ganyu*?[15]

(e) How many hours in the last seven days did you engage in casual, part-time or ganyu labor?

(f) How many hours in the last seven days did you help in any of the household's nonagricultural or non-fishing household businesses, if any?

(g) How many hours in the last seven days did you run or do any kind of nonagricultural or non-fishing household business, big or small, for yourself?

When computing the total time of work, the individual-level indicator is the sum of the time spent by individuals in the various categories of work identified in the survey, whether this time is spent in the labor market, for domestic chores or for collecting water and wood. The absence of questions in the survey on the time spent by individuals caring for children, sick household members and disabled people makes it likely that our estimates of the total workload of individuals are too low, but this bias need not be very large if it many activities related to care are carried on as secondary activities in combination with other activities (such as cooking, cleaning, or making laundry) that are recorded in the survey.[16] Another limitation of the data is that there is a single question for all domestic chores (cooking, laundry, and cleaning) apart from water and wood collection, which is likely to lead to some noise in the data. Yet, given that we are focusing in this paper on the seasonality of time use, and that domestic chores are not likely to have the same degree of seasonality as labor-related activities, the potential errors of measurement for domestic work time are less serious.

Figure 5.1 provides the distribution of total individual working hours per week for adults (individuals aged 15 and above). Hours have been aggregated into hour worked in the last seven days (where daily hour non-income generating work is multiplied by seven). The four graphs account respectively for men and women, as well as urban and rural areas. Clearly, rural individuals work longer hours than urban individuals, and women work more than men. Mean values for the number of hours worked are given at the national level and in rural areas by quintile of consumption per equivalent adult and by month in Tables 5.3 and 5.4 for both the adult population and children. The mean working time year-round nationally is 36.4 hours per week for the adult population (above 15 years of age) and a much lower 8.5 hours for children. In rural areas, where 88 percent of the population lives, the mean values are slightly higher.

What is most important for our purpose is the seasonality evident in Tables 5.5 and 5.6. For the adult population, the average level of working hours is peaking in December–January, which is as discussed earlier, the busy part of the cropping season. At that time, the adult population works on average more than five hours more per week than the annual mean. The seasonal differential in working hours is largest for the individuals who belong to the poorest quintile of the distribution of consumption per capita. In rural areas, the

---

15. *Ganyu* refers to short-term, temporary rural daily labor.

16. Malawi is facing one of the world's most severe HIV/AIDS Pandemics. With an estimated prevalence rate of 14.2 percent, it ranks eighth in the world (Population Reference Bureau 2004).

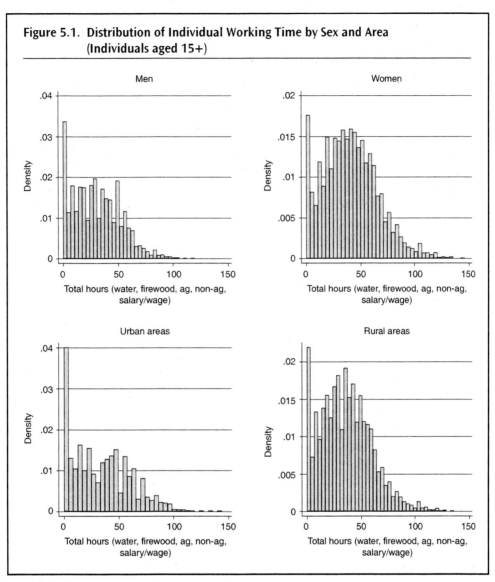

Figure 5.1. Distribution of Individual Working Time by Sex and Area (Individuals aged 15+)

Source: Authors' estimation using IHS2.

additional workload in December compared to the annual average amounts to close to 10 hours in the first quintile. December is also the busiest month of the year for children.

Tables 5.5 and 5.6 provide additional information by showing the distribution of hours of work according to the type of work performed and the gender of the individual. As expected, adult men spend more time in the labor market than adult women, essentially because of a larger average amount of time given to salaried work, as well as casual, part-time and *ganyu* work and non-agricultural business-related work. On the other hand, the differences between adult men and women in terms of the time spent on agricultural work

Table 5.3. Total Time Spent Working by Area and Consumption Quintile, National Sample

	Poorest Quintile	2nd Quintile	3rd Quintile	4th Quintile	Richest Quintile	Total
	National, adults (Age 15 and over)					
March 2004	34.0	32.6	36.0	35.6	38.4	35.7
April 2004	34.1	34.7	35.6	35.7	37.8	35.8
May 2004	28.3	31.7	33.7	34.5	38.3	33.8
June 2004	34.0	33.2	35.6	36.0	35.4	35.1
July 2004	28.4	33.1	32.2	34.4	35.2	33.5
August 2004	33.3	34.9	33.2	32.9	36.3	34.3
September 2004	34.5	35.5	35.4	38.3	34.5	35.7
October 2004	34.9	39.2	38.5	38.6	37.5	37.6
November 2004	39.8	40.2	40.3	38.1	40.3	39.8
December 2004	44.5	42.1	42.1	37.9	41.3	41.7
January 2005	38.9	41.1	43.1	41.1	42.1	41.2
February 2005	35.1	36.1	37.6	38.8	35.3	36.5
March 2005	33.8	38.5	36.7	36.2	41.2	37.0
Annual average	35.0	36.2	36.5	36.3	37.5	36.4
	National, children (Below 15 years old)					
March 2004	8.0	7.7	6.9	8.5	8.5	7.9
April 2004	9.5	10.7	9.9	10.4	10.1	10.2
May 2004	5.6	7.8	7.3	9.8	6.4	7.3
June 2004	5.3	6.8	8.3	7.9	7.4	7.2
July 2004	5.4	7.2	7.5	8.6	7.8	7.6
August 2004	8.3	9.7	9.8	9.3	10.8	9.6
September 2004	6.8	8.2	7.3	8.2	7.2	7.5
October 2004	7.4	8.4	8.6	6.9	7.6	7.8
November 2004	8.3	9.6	8.6	10.9	8.1	9.0
December 2004	12.8	12.3	13.2	15.4	11.3	12.9
January 2005	8.8	7.7	7.9	7.8	7.6	8.1
February 2005	7.4	8.2	9.0	9.4	7.3	8.1
March 2005	6.5	10.1	7.6	10.4	12.4	8.5
Annual average	7.7	8.9	8.6	9.3	8.6	8.5

Source: Authors' estimation using 2004 HIS.

are more limited on average (all values in the tables include zero values). As for domestic work, it is performed mostly by women, and the same holds for the collection of wood and water. In total, the mean and median working hours for women are about 10 hours above the corresponding values for men at the national level.

Table 5.4. Total Time Spent Working by Area and Consumption Quintile, Rural Areas

	Poorest Quintile	2nd Quintile	3rd Quintile	4th Quintile	Richest Quintile	Total
	Rural areas, adults (Age 15 and over)					
March 2004	34.3	32.9	36.4	37.3	39.5	36.3
April 2004	34.1	34.8	36.0	36.2	38.4	36.1
May 2004	29.0	31.8	35.0	34.8	38.2	33.8
June 2004	34.0	33.3	36.1	36.1	35.7	35.2
July 2004	27.4	33.1	31.9	34.8	35.6	33.6
August 2004	33.7	34.6	32.9	32.7	35.4	33.9
September 2004	33.7	35.0	35.0	37.9	35.7	35.6
October 2004	35.1	39.3	38.7	37.8	38.8	37.8
November 2004	40.1	40.7	41.2	39.4	41.5	40.6
December 2004	45.0	42.9	43.1	38.5	42.0	42.5
January 2005	39.1	40.2	41.5	41.4	44.2	41.1
February 2005	35.5	36.6	38.2	38.8	35.1	36.8
March 2005	34.3	38.2	37.5	35.9	40.2	36.9
Annual average	35.2	36.2	36.8	36.5	37.8	36.5
	Rural areas, children (Below 15 years old)					
March 2004	8.1	7.9	7.2	9.4	9.8	8.4
April 2004	9.6	11.0	10.0	10.8	10.9	10.4
May 2004	5.7	7.9	7.4	9.8	6.9	7.4
June 2004	5.3	6.4	8.2	7.7	7.9	7.1
July 2004	5.2	7.0	7.5	9.0	8.0	7.7
August 2004	8.5	9.6	9.8	8.8	11.2	9.5
September 2004	6.8	7.7	6.4	8.1	7.5	7.2
October 2004	7.5	8.5	8.7	6.5	9.2	8.0
November 2004	8.3	9.5	8.9	12.3	6.9	9.2
December 2004	12.9	12.3	15.0	15.5	8.7	13.2
January 2005	7.9	7.7	7.8	7.5	9.5	7.9
February 2005	7.6	8.3	8.4	6.2	6.5	7.8
March 2005	6.8	10.0	7.3	7.4	7.5	8.0
Annual average	7.8	8.8	8.5	9.1	8.9	8.5

Source: Authors' estimation using 2004 HIS.

As we expect gender and seasonality issues to be more pronounced in rural households, Tables 5.7 and 5.8 focus on the population residing in rural areas. The gender differences are even larger, at 11.0 hours for the median, and 11.6 hours for the mean. The workloads for children are much lower, but girls do work longer hours than boys, again mainly due to a higher burden from domestic work as well as water collection.

Table 5.5. Work Time by Gender, Month, and Age According to the Categories of Time Recorded in the Survey, Malawi–National, 2004

	Cooking, laundry, and cleaning	Collecting water	Collecting fire-wood	Agricultural work	Running non-ag. business	Helping for non-ag. business	Casual, part-time & ganyu work	Salaried work	Total work (mean)	Total work (median)	Working less than 10 hours	Working more than 70 hours
Adult males (age 15 and over), national												
March 2004	1.6	0.5	0.5	13.9	3.4	0.7	2.5	6.0	29.1	24.5	27.4	8.0
April 2004	1.9	0.6	0.5	13.5	5.4	0.7	2.5	6.3	31.5	30.0	18.0	7.3
May 2004	1.9	0.6	0.3	11.8	4.5	0.8	1.8	6.6	28.3	26.0	24.3	5.4
June 2004	1.9	0.9	0.3	10.9	3.8	0.7	2.5	8.5	29.6	30.0	22.0	4.7
July 2004	2.2	0.9	0.6	10.5	5.4	0.5	3.2	5.7	29.0	27.0	19.7	5.3
August 2004	2.4	0.7	0.3	10.7	5.7	0.4	2.5	6.0	28.6	25.0	21.8	5.4
Sept. 2004	2.7	0.8	0.4	10.8	3.9	0.4	3.0	9.0	31.0	28.0	19.6	7.7
Oct. 2004	2.2	0.6	0.3	13.8	4.1	0.2	3.4	6.4	31.1	30.0	17.7	6.5
Nov. 2004	2.6	0.7	0.4	15.8	3.0	0.2	2.7	8.9	34.4	34.0	12.3	7.6
Dec. 2004	1.8	0.6	0.3	20.6	4.2	0.3	3.2	5.7	36.7	36.0	6.8	6.5
Jan. 2005	2.4	1.0	0.3	18.5	3.4	0.1	2.5	7.6	35.9	35.0	8.8	9.2
Feb. 2005	1.8	0.7	0.3	15.6	3.1	0.2	2.2	6.7	30.6	30.0	16.1	4.5
March 2005	2.4	0.7	0.3	14.2	3.9	0.5	2.6	7.5	32.2	30.0	16.3	7.1
Adult females (age 15 and over), national												
March 2004	14.8	5.3	3.0	12.5	2.2	1.1	1.7	1.4	41.9	38.0	11.8	17.4
April 2004	14.0	5.1	2.1	13.0	2.5	0.6	1.2	1.2	39.8	37.0	11.8	12.9
May 2004	13.6	5.4	2.3	13.2	1.6	0.6	1.0	1.3	39.0	38.0	10.9	10.9
June 2004	15.0	6.1	2.3	11.0	2.3	0.5	1.7	1.5	40.3	38.0	10.7	14.4

July 2004	14.5	6.4	2.4	8.6	2.6	0.3	1.6	1.2	37.7	35.0	11.5	10.9
August 2004	15.3	7.0	2.3	9.6	3.0	0.2	1.0	1.1	39.6	37.0	8.1	11.6
Sept. 2004	15.2	6.9	2.1	11.0	2.5	0.4	0.9	1.2	40.3	38.5	9.6	12.8
Oct. 2004	15.3	6.9	2.1	14.6	2.0	0.3	1.0	1.6	43.7	43.0	7.7	12.1
Nov. 2004	14.6	6.7	2.0	16.4	1.6	0.3	1.3	2.3	45.2	45.0	7.1	14.6
Dec. 2004	13.6	5.9	1.6	20.2	1.6	0.2	1.7	1.0	45.9	45.5	6.3	12.2
Jan. 2005	14.2	7.8	2.0	17.4	1.0	0.5	1.2	1.8	45.9	46.0	7.4	13.1
Feb. 2005	14.1	6.4	1.7	15.1	1.3	0.2	1.6	1.2	41.9	41.5	8.5	11.3
March 2005	14.7	6.8	2.1	13.2	1.5	0.3	1.3	1.6	41.5	40.5	6.9	10.1

Source: Authors' estimation using 2004 HIS.

Table 5.6. Work Time by Gender, Month, and Age According to the Categories of Time Recorded in the Survey, Malawi–National, 2004

	Cooking, laundry, and cleaning	Collecting water	Collecting fire-wood	Agricultural work	Running non-ag. business	Helping for non-ag. business	Casual, part-time & ganyu work	Salaried work	Total work (mean)	Total work (median)	Working less than 10 hours	Working more than 70 hours
	Boys (age 5 to 14), national											
March 2004	1.0	0.8	0.1	2.4	0.2	0.2	0.2	0.2	5.3	0.0	77.9	2.9
April 2004	1.3	1.0	0.3	4.5	0.1	0.2	0.3	0.1	7.8	3.0	71.0	2.6
May 2004	1.2	0.9	0.5	2.4	0.2	0.1	0.3	0.1	5.6	0.5	77.8	2.0
June 2004	1.6	1.2	0.4	2.3	0.1	0.1	0.2	0.1	6.0	0.5	76.9	2.2
July 2004	1.0	1.3	0.2	1.8	0.1	0.3	0.4	0.2	5.3	0.0	79.5	1.0
August 2004	1.9	1.4	0.3	3.0	0.0	0.2	0.2	0.2	7.2	0.0	68.7	2.2
Sept. 2004	2.1	1.2	0.2	1.9	0.0	0.0	0.2	0.1	5.8	0.0	77.6	2.0
Oct. 2004	1.1	1.0	0.2	2.8	0.0	0.1	0.3	0.0	5.5	0.0	79.6	1.1
Nov. 2004	1.8	0.9	0.3	4.1	0.0	0.0	0.3	0.1	7.5	1.0	72.5	2.3
Dec. 2004	1.6	1.1	0.4	6.8	0.1	0.0	0.8	0.1	10.9	3.5	60.0	1.1
Jan. 2005	1.3	1.1	0.1	2.7	0.0	0.1	0.2	0.0	5.5	0.0	74.2	0.6
Feb. 2005	1.5	1.1	0.2	3.3	0.0	0.0	0.3	0.1	6.6	0.0	77.4	1.3
March 2005	2.0	1.0	0.3	2.5	0.1	0.0	0.2	0.2	6.4	0.0	78.5	1.3
	Girls (age 5 to 14), national											
March 2004	3.4	3.0	0.8	2.1	0.3	0.6	0.3	0.3	10.7	4.5	61.3	3.0
April 2004	3.8	3.4	1.1	3.3	0.2	0.4	0.2	0.0	12.5	7.0	58.2	2.7
May 2004	3.2	3.0	0.7	1.9	0.1	0.1	0.2	0.0	9.2	7.0	61.6	1.3
June 2004	3.1	2.6	0.7	1.3	0.1	0.2	0.3	0.2	8.4	3.5	67.7	1.4

July 2004	3.4	3.5	1.0	1.0	0.1	0.4	0.4	0.0	9.7	4.5	64.9	0.9
August 2004	4.4	4.1	0.8	1.9	0.0	0.3	0.1	0.1	11.8	7.0	56.1	2.6
Sept. 2004	3.5	3.4	0.8	1.0	0.0	0.2	0.0	0.1	9.1	7.0	62.1	2.0
Oct. 2004	3.4	3.3	1.0	2.1	0.1	0.1	0.1	0.0	10.0	7.0	62.3	1.4
Nov. 2004	3.5	3.1	0.6	2.9	0.0	0.1	0.0	0.5	10.6	7.0	59.9	2.1
Dec. 2004	4.3	3.3	1.0	5.9	0.1	0.0	0.6	0.0	15.2	10.0	49.5	0.9
Jan. 2005	2.9	3.6	0.4	3.3	0.1	0.0	0.2	0.0	10.6	7.0	58.6	0.6
Feb. 2005	2.9	3.3	0.5	2.8	0.0	0.0	0.1	0.0	9.7	3.5	67.1	1.1
March 2005	4.2	2.8	0.7	2.6	0.0	0.0	0.1	0.3	10.7	3.5	67.3	3.2

Source: Authors' estimation using 2004 HIS.

Table 5.7. Work Time by Gender, Month, and Age According to the Categories of Time Recorded in the Survey, Malawi–Rural, 2004

	Cooking laundry, and cleaning	Collecting water	Collecting firewood	Agricultural work	Running non-ag. business	Helping for non-ag. business	Casual, part-time & ganyu work	Salaried work	Total work (mean)	Total work (median)	Working less than 10 hours	Working more than 70 hours
				Adult males (age 15 and over), rural								
March 2004	1.5	0.5	0.6	15.6	2.6	0.7	2.6	4.9	29.0	25.0	26.4	8.1
April 2004	1.7	0.6	0.5	15.2	5.9	0.7	2.5	3.6	30.9	29.0	17.2	6.9
May 2004	1.5	0.6	0.4	13.9	3.6	0.5	1.9	4.7	27.0	25.0	24.2	4.8
June 2004	1.6	0.9	0.4	12.6	3.3	0.7	2.6	6.1	28.3	28.0	22.0	4.7
July 2004	2.1	0.8	0.6	11.2	4.9	0.6	2.9	5.1	28.3	26.0	19.1	4.9
August 2004	2.2	0.7	0.3	12.2	4.4	0.3	2.4	4.4	26.9	24.0	22.2	4.6
Sept. 2004	2.4	0.8	0.4	12.8	3.6	0.2	2.7	6.7	29.4	26.0	18.4	7.0
Oct. 2004	1.9	0.6	0.3	15.5	4.0	0.2	3.4	4.5	30.3	30.0	16.5	5.8
Nov. 2004	2.1	0.7	0.4	18.8	2.2	0.2	3.1	6.3	33.9	32.0	10.9	6.8
Dec. 2004	1.3	0.6	0.3	24.7	2.8	0.3	3.1	3.0	36.2	34.5	4.0	5.5
Jan. 2005	1.5	0.9	0.3	19.4	3.4	0.1	2.4	7.1	35.2	34.5	7.4	7.4
Feb. 2005	1.6	0.7	0.3	16.7	3.0	0.2	2.3	5.2	29.9	28.0	15.7	4.3
March 2005	1.9	0.8	0.3	16.3	3.3	0.2	2.8	5.2	30.8	30.0	15.6	5.2
				Adult females (age 15 and over), rural								
March 2004	14.7	5.6	3.3	13.6	1.9	1.2	1.8	0.8	43.0	38.5	10.5	18.1
April 2004	14.0	5.4	2.2	14.1	2.4	0.6	1.1	0.9	40.7	38.5	10.8	13.2
May 2004	13.6	5.8	2.6	14.8	1.3	0.3	1.1	0.4	39.9	38.5	8.6	10.4
June 2004	15.1	6.7	2.6	12.4	2.0	0.5	1.9	0.4	41.7	39.5	9.5	14.6

July 2004	14.5	6.7	2.5	9.3	2.4	0.4	1.6	1.2	38.5	35.0	11.1	11.1
August 2004	15.4	7.3	2.5	10.6	2.5	0.2	1.0	0.6	40.2	38.0	7.6	11.3
Sept. 2004	15.4	7.4	2.4	12.4	2.1	0.4	0.8	0.5	41.4	40.0	8.9	13.0
Oct. 2004	15.3	7.4	2.3	15.8	1.7	0.3	1.1	0.7	44.6	44.0	6.9	12.5
Nov. 2004	14.3	7.4	2.3	19.0	1.2	0.3	1.5	1.1	47.2	46.0	5.2	15.0
Dec. 2004	12.6	6.4	1.8	23.3	1.0	0.2	2.0	0.4	47.7	47.0	4.5	12.1
Jan. 2005	13.8	8.2	1.9	18.2	0.9	0.5	1.0	1.7	46.4	47.0	5.5	12.9
Feb. 2005	14.0	6.8	1.8	15.9	1.3	0.3	1.7	1.2	43.1	43.0	7.4	11.6
March 2005	14.0	7.3	2.2	14.8	1.4	0.2	1.5	1.0	42.4	41.0	6.8	10.3

Source: Authors' estimation using 2004 HIS.

Table 5.8. Work Time by Gender, Month, and Age According to the Categories of Time Recorded in the Survey, Malawi – Rural, 2004

	Cooking laundry, and cleaning	Collecting water	Collecting fire-wood	Agricultural work	Running non-ag. business	Helping for non-ag. business	Casual, part-time & ganyu work	Salaried work	Total work (mean)	Total work (median)	Working less than 10 hours	Working more than 70 hours
Boys (age 5 to 15), rural												
March 2004	0.9	0.9	0.1	2.7	0.2	0.3	0.3	0.3	5.6	0.0	76.6	3.2
April 2004	1.2	1.0	0.3	4.7	0.1	0.3	0.3	0.1	8.0	3.0	70.5	2.6
May 2004	0.9	0.9	0.5	2.6	0.3	0.1	0.3	0.1	5.6	0.0	78.0	2.3
June 2004	1.1	1.3	0.4	2.5	0.1	0.1	0.2	0.1	5.7	0.0	77.9	2.1
July 2004	1.0	1.4	0.2	1.9	0.1	0.2	0.5	0.2	5.6	0.0	78.8	0.7
August 2004	1.3	1.4	0.3	3.2	0.0	0.2	0.2	0.2	6.9	0.0	70.0	2.1
Sept. 2004	1.3	1.2	0.2	2.1	0.1	0.1	0.2	0.2	5.3	0.0	79.3	2.3
Oct. 2004	0.9	1.0	0.2	3.0	0.0	0.1	0.3	0.0	5.6	0.0	79.8	0.7
Nov. 2004	1.5	0.9	0.3	4.5	0.0	0.0	0.3	0.1	7.6	2.0	72.4	2.4
Dec. 2004	0.9	1.2	0.4	7.7	0.1	0.0	0.9	0.1	11.3	4.0	58.5	1.1
Jan. 2005	0.8	1.2	0.1	2.7	0.0	0.2	0.1	0.0	5.0	0.0	75.8	0.7
Feb. 2005	0.8	1.2	0.2	3.5	0.0	0.1	0.3	0.0	6.1	0.0	78.0	1.4
March 2005	1.2	1.0	0.4	2.7	0.1	0.0	0.2	0.2	6.0	0.0	78.9	1.2
Girls (age 5 to 15), rural												
March 2004	3.6	3.2	0.9	2.2	0.3	0.6	0.3	0.3	11.3	6.0	58.9	3.1
April 2004	3.8	3.5	1.2	3.6	0.2	0.5	0.2	0.0	13.0	7.0	57.5	2.4
May 2004	3.0	3.2	0.8	2.1	0.1	0.1	0.2	0.0	9.4	7.0	60.7	1.4
June 2004	2.7	2.9	0.8	1.4	0.1	0.1	0.4	0.1	8.4	3.5	67.5	1.3

July 2004	3.3	3.5	1.0	1.0	0.1	0.2	0.5	0.0	9.7	4.5	65.1	1.0
August 2004	4.0	4.4	0.9	2.1	0.0	0.3	0.1	0.1	12.1	7.0	56.0	2.7
Sept. 2004	2.9	3.7	0.9	1.2	0.0	0.2	0.0	0.1	9.0	7.0	62.9	1.9
Oct. 2004	3.3	3.4	1.1	2.2	0.2	0.1	0.1	0.0	10.3	7.0	61.2	1.4
Nov. 2004	3.2	3.4	0.7	3.3	0.0	0.1	0.0	0.1	10.8	7.0	57.4	1.7
Dec. 2004	3.0	3.6	1.1	6.9	0.1	0.0	0.7	0.0	15.4	10.5	49.0	0.7
Jan. 2005	2.5	3.8	0.4	3.2	0.1	0.0	0.1	0.0	10.3	7.0	58.9	0.7
Feb. 2005	2.3	3.5	0.6	2.9	0.0	0.0	0.1	0.0	9.4	3.5	67.1	1.2
March 2005	3.2	3.0	0.9	2.8	0.0	0.0	0.1	0.1	10.1	3.5	66.7	3.1

Source: Authors' estimation using 2004 HIS.

As noted by Bardasi and Wodon (2005), the concept of time poverty can be used to measure the share of the population that works very long hours, and can therefore be considered as time-poor. In their paper on Guinea, Bardasi and Wodon consider a time poverty line of about 70 hours per week. A similar threshold has been used in Tables 5.5–5.8 to measure the share of the population working at least 70 hours per week. In rural areas, as shown in Table 5.7, on an annual basis 5.2 percent of the adult male population works more than 70 hours per week, while the proportion is 10.3 percent for women. Interestingly, there is no clear seasonal pattern in the share of the population working more than 70 hours per week, suggesting that the overall increase in working hours observed around December–January is likely to be provided by those household members that have a reserve of time at their disposal rather than by those who already work the most.

While a small share of the population in Malawi can be considered as time poor according to the data in Tables 5.5–5.8, a larger share can be considered as underemployed, at least in the case of men. On an annual basis, 15.6 percent of adult males work less than 10 hours per week, and this proportion peaks to more than 20 percent in some months. For women, the proportion working less than 10 hours per week is much smaller. Importantly, we do see the impact of seasonality in this measure of underemployment, since the proportion of adults working less than 10 hours per week is lowest again in December. The corresponding data for children suggest a much larger share with a small burden of work, but also some cases apparently of very high workload.

Looking more closely at rural households, we examine to what extent land holdings per adult are associated with seasonal labor constraints. The indicator of the seasonality of labor is the ratio of mean adult hours in the peak months (December–January) to the surplus months (May–July). This is a crude measure, as peak and surplus months will vary across regions (as described in the introduction and shown in Tables 5.1 and 5.2). Nonetheless, even with this imprecise measure we find evidence that seasonality affects small land holders the most. Figure 5.2 shows that seasonal labor issues are most pronounced for the smaller holders with less than 0.15 hectares of land per adult. Among these small land holding households, mean hours in December–January are more than 35 percent higher than the corresponding measure during the surplus labor season. For other land categories, including households with no land holdings and those with large holdings, we also see seasonality. For landless households, this will reflect land demand for *ganyu* workers during planting seasons. In turn, it is the larger land holders who hire such labor,[17] which explains the lower ratio of peak-to-surplus season hours for the large holders.

Conclusion

With a population density of 112 people per square kilometer, Malawi has the highest population density among neighboring countries. Generally, labor in Malawi is assumed to be

---

17. While the prevalence of hiring labor at least for one day on rain-fed plots is even across the land categories in Figure 5.2, the intensity of such labor is not even. The number of days of hired labor increases significantly as land holdings increase.

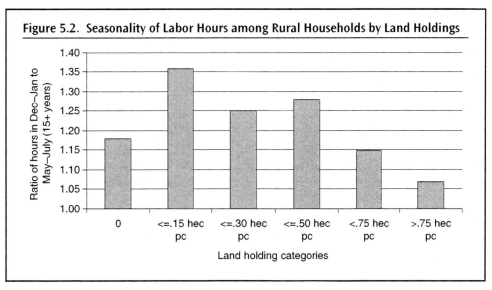

Figure 5.2. **Seasonality of Labor Hours among Rural Households by Land Holdings**

Source: Authors' estimation using 2004 HIS.

in surplus supply, with extensive underemployment. However, low mean hours in income-generating activities mask the existence of labor shortages at the peak of the cropping season. This seasonality in labor supply can have potentially large negative impacts on the ability of households to make the most of their endowments such as land as well as their labor. Using data from 2004 collected from households over a 13-month period, this paper has documented the extent to which the seasonality in the demand for labor is leading to both underemployment and labor shortages.

Defining work broadly to include income-generating activities (including work on the household farm) as well as main household chores (including fetching firewood and water), we find typical labor supply patterns. The population in rural areas works longer hours than urban individuals, and women work more than men. Across activities, while men have higher hours in income-generating work, chores (including firewood and water collection) are more extensively done by women such that their total hours are higher. The seasonal differential in working hours is largest for individuals who belong to the poorest quintile of the distribution of consumption per capita. As alternative to consumption wealth, the paper also examined seasonal differences by household landholdings. Small holders had the largest seasonal differences, with mean hours in peak month 35 percent higher than surplus months.

Understanding the implications of these patterns will require additional analysis, but the results suggest that the precious few endowments of poor households (labor and land) may not be utilized in the most efficient way, or at least, it can be argued that there are serious constraints to the generation of higher earnings for households, despite the presence of underemployment for most of the year. Poverty reduction strategies would need to take into account the strong seasonal dimensions to labor supply to be effective.

References

Bardasi, E., and Q. Wodon. 2005. "Measuring Time Poverty and Analyzing its Determinants: Concepts and Application to Guinea." (Chapter 4 in this volume.)

Beegle, K. 2005. "Labor Effects of Adult Mortality in Tanzanian Households." *Economic Development and Cultural Change* 53:655–684.

Brummett, R.E. 2002. "Seasonality, Labor and Integration of Aquaculture into Southern African Smallhold Farming Systems." *Naga - The ICLARM Quarterly*, 25(1).

Dercon, S., and P. Krishnan. 2000. "Vulnerability, Seasonality and Poverty in Ethiopia." *Journal of Development Studies* 36:25–53.

Ellis, F. 2000. "The Determinants of Rural Livelihood Diversification in Developing Countries." *Journal of Agricultural Economics* 51:289–302.

Kamanga, B.C.G. 2002. *Understanding the Farmer's Agricultural Environment in Malawi.* Risk Management Projects Working Paper Series 02-01, International Maize and Wheat Improvement Center, Mexico.

Kanwar, S. 2004. "Seasonality and Wage Responsiveness in a Developing Agrarian Economy." *Oxford Bulletin of Economics and Statistics* 66:189–204.

Pitt, M.M., and S. Khandker. 2002. "Credit Programmes for the Poor and Seasonality in Rural Bangladesh." *Journal of Development Studies* 39:1–24.

Population Reference Bureau. 2004. "Top 15 HIV/AIDS Prevalence Countries (end 2003)."

Shah, M.K., N. Osborne, T. Mbilizi, and G. Vilili. 2001. *Impact of HIV/AIDS on Agricultural Productivity and Rural Livelihoods in the Central Region of Malawi.* CARE International, Malawi.

Skoufias, E. 1993. "Seasonal Labor Utilization in Agriculture: Theory and Evidence from Agrarian Households in India." *American Journal of Agricultural Economics* 75:20–32.

Skoufias, E. 1994. "Risk and Seasonality in an Empirical Model of the Farm Household." *Journal of Economic Development* 19:93–116.

Tango International. 2003. *Malawi Baseline Survey: Report of Findings.* C-Safe.

PART III

Time Use and Development Outcomes

CHAPTER 6

Poverty Reduction from Full Employment: A Time Use Approach

Elena Bardasi and Quentin Wodon[18]

Despite long working hours, for many household members, and especially women, underemployment is nevertheless affecting a large share of the population in many developing countries. Using data on time use, wages, and consumption levels from a recent household survey for Guinea, this paper provides a simple framework for assessing the potential impact on poverty and inequality of an increase in the working hours of the population up to what is referred to as a full employment workload. The framework provides for a decomposition of the contribution to higher household consumption of an increase in working hours for both men and women. The key message is that job creation and full employment would lead to a significant reduction in poverty, even at the relatively low current levels of wages and earnings enjoyed by the population. However, even at full employment levels, poverty would remain massive, and the higher workload that the full employment scenario would entail would be significant.

According to economic theory, individuals spend more time in work to achieve a higher level of utility, based on the budget constraint they face and their preferences for work and leisure. By extension, they allocate time between labor market and household production based on the returns they can obtain in the two domains. However, because markets are far from perfect, and because various individuals and households

18. The authors are with the World Bank. This work was prepared as a contribution to the Poverty Assessment for Guinea prepared at the World Bank. The authors acknowledge support from the Trust Fund ESSDD as well as the Belgian Poverty Reduction Partnership for research on this issue as part of a small research program on gender, time use and poverty in Sub-Saharan Africa which also benefited from funding from the GENFUND. Preliminary results from the paper were presented at a three-day workshop organized in Guinea in October 2005 in collaboration with the country's National Statistical Office (*Direction Nationale de la Statistique*), and at a World Bank workshop in November 2005. We are grateful to Kathleen Beegle and Mark Blackden for comments. The views expressed here are those of the authors and need not reflect those of the World Bank, its Executive Directors or the countries they represent.

have different endowments, reality is different. Although we may expect more time in work (especially more time spent in the labor market) to be associated with higher consumption, empirical evidence indicates that "vulnerable" categories, such as women and low educated people, often work very long hours for very little output and that for these groups a lack of time to perform any additional work and poverty itself may go together. This occurs when the available technology is so poor that very labor-intensive activities are required to reach a minimum subsistence level. The consequence is that not only are long hours spent to achieve little output (as measured through production, income, or consumption)—in effect, the productivity of one working hour is low—but, because of the long hours already worked, few additional time resources are available to increase consumption (or income) further.

The difficult situation of labor markets for the poor in Sub-Saharan Africa and many other developing areas in terms of both low productivity (low earnings per hour of work) and limited time available for productive work are due to a complex range of factors. On the time constraint side, the lack of access to basic infrastructure services means that households spend a lot of time in domestic chores and for fetching wood and water (see Chapter 3 for a review of the empirical evidence on time use in Africa). On the productivity or earnings potential side, there has been a process of informalization in many countries, with in some cases a gap arising between the education received by young adults and the requirements of the job opportunities available to them (see for example Calves and Schoumaker 2004 on urban Burkina Faso). Furthermore, given that many African countries have suffered from low rates of economic growth, the economic opportunities for emerging from poverty through hard work have been limited.

If many among the poor already work long hours and if their productivity is limited, is it correct to state that the main asset of the poor to fight poverty is their labor? Not necessarily, or at least not in a necessarily straightforward way. It is clear that the poor in Africa derive their livelihood from their labor, and in that sense, it is indeed correct to state that their main asset to emerge from poverty is their labor. However, it is not as clear that labor is abundant and systematically underused (Blackden and Bhanu 1999), and it is also not fully clear whether an increase in the supply of labor by the poor would actually help in a significant way to reduce poverty since the productivity of the poor is constrained in many ways, especially among female headed households (Buvinic and Rao Gupta 1997), but also more generally.[19] The answer to these two questions must essentially be settled empirically as conditions may differ between countries.

In practice, in order to analyze the potential for poverty reduction from full employment, it is useful to rely on a time use approach in order to estimate for the individual what would be the level of a reasonable increase in labor supply that could be provided by household members without reaching such high levels of work as to become time poor (this idea follows Bardasi and Wodon 2005). The objective of this paper is thus to provide a simple framework for analyzing these questions, and apply the framework to recent household survey data from Guinea. Although we do recognize that substantial long-term increases

---

19. Buvinic and Rao Gupta (1997) argue that poverty is often higher among female-headed households not only because of higher dependency ratios, but also because of lack of economic opportunities and low wages for women.

in standards of living in countries such as Guinea will probably need to come first from higher productivity that would lead to higher wages and earnings per hour of work, we focus in this paper solely on the potential for poverty reduction from full employment at current wages and productivity levels. That is, we answer the question: by what magnitude would poverty be reduced under full employment, assuming that higher working hours would be remunerated at their current level?

The basic idea of the paper is to measure how much additional income or consumption could be obtained by households if all their members who are currently working fewer hours than a certain threshold were working a number of hours corresponding to that threshold. Although we are aware of the issue of seasonality in time use and work patterns, we do not discuss here the question of the impact of seasonality on labor demand and supply.[20] We also do not consider the issue of what exactly individuals would do if they worked more—although it is clear that households tend to adopt multiple livelihood strategies with diversified rural livelihoods leading to a reduction in vulnerability (Ellis 2000), we simply assume here that additional hours of work are paid at the same wage or productivity rate as the hours currently worked by individual household members. Finally, we do not look at whether there is in fact a labor demand out there that could absorb the additional working hours that individuals would be willing to work (in India, Kanwar [2004] analyzes how labor supply and demand respond to wages in the agricultural market for daily-rated labor, suggesting excess supply in the post-rainy season.)

The very simple framework provided in this paper is limited, but it does enable the analysis of the potential impact of full employment at current wages and productivity on poverty to be conducted for the population as a whole as well as by gender, with a number of tests for the robustness of the results to the assumptions made. The next section presents the data we use. The two sections after that present the framework and the empirical results. The final section draws conclusions.

Data

The data we use come from the *Enquête Intégrée de base pour l'évaluation de la pauvreté* (EIBEP) of Guinea, year 2002–2003. Section 4 of the questionnaire includes a section where each individual aged 6 and over is requested to report the time spent in the week before the interview for a set of domestic tasks (cooking, cleaning, laundry, ironing, going to the market), fetching water, fetching wood, helping other households and being involved in community activities. In the same section other questions aim to record the amount of time the individual spent working in the labor market, for a wage (as an employee) or in a farm or family business (as a self-employed or contributing family member). We used these data to compute the total time spent by individuals in work of any type (domestic work and work in the labor market, whether paid or unpaid).

Three caveats are in order regarding the data used. The data were collected retrospectively for the week before the interview. Such data are, according to many researchers, not

---

20. On seasonality, see for example Skoufias (1993); Dercon and Krishnan (2000); and Wodon and Beegle (2005).

the best quality data to study time use—diaries generate more accurate data. Moreover (and related to this), simultaneous activities are not counted; however this is perhaps not a major problem when the interest is—as in our case—in the total time spent in work. Finally, there is no information in the questionnaire about caring activities (time spent caring for children, old, sick, and disabled people); however, we can probably assume that these activities are in large part usually performed as a "secondary activity" in combination with one of the other activities recorded in the questionnaire.

As discussed in the companion paper in this volume by Bardasi and Wodon (2005), we have created two definitions of the total time spent in work. The first definition includes the total amount of time spent by the individual in the labor market, in domestic chores and in collecting water and wood. The second definition adds to the first the amount of time spent helping other households and in community activities. One may argue that spending time helping other households and in community activities has more of a "choice" than of a "duty" connotation—it could be seen as a use of leisure rather than "work." For this reason, we excluded this use of time helping other households and in community activities from the total time spent "in work" here.

Table 6.1 shows the average amount of time spent by adult individuals (15 years of age and above) in various activities, by quintile of consumption per person and in rural and urban areas. First, individuals in the top quintiles spend slightly *more* time in all type of work than poorer individuals. This is true in both urban and rural areas. The only exception is represented by work in a farm or family business, in which poor people spend longer hours than rich people. However, this trend is more than compensated by the pattern of hours spent working for a wage —in this case hours are much longer in the top than in the bottom of the consumption distribution, so that the overall time spent in the labor market tends to be higher in the top quintiles (with the exception of the rural areas, where it is almost the same in every quintile). Second, the differences between urban and rural areas tend to be larger than across consumption quintiles; in particular, the time spent in the labor market and the time spent fetching water and wood is higher in rural than in urban areas. Third, the differences across quintiles are more pronounced in urban than in rural areas. Looking at the differences in total time (according to our first definition), the average adult individual in the top quintile spent about 39 hours in employment in urban area and 49 in rural area, while in the bottom of the distribution the average time in employment was 31 and 48 hours respectively (these figures include the zeros).

Analytical Framework

Table 6.1 above hides a lot of heterogeneity. While many individuals work very long hours, others are clearly underemployed and could potentially increase the amount of time they work to increase the well-being of their household. In what follows, we conduct simulations to try to measure the loss in consumption or income associated with underemployment for the individuals in our sample. We assume that each adult individual who is working less than a certain number of hours per week could increase his or her working time up to that level in order to increase the level of consumption of the household members, while all the other members who are at or above the time poverty line continue working the

Table 6.1. Working Time per Week, Adult Population by Consumption Quintile and Location

	1	2	3	4	5
	Urban				
1 Cooking	2.6	3.0	3.0	3.5	3.8
2 Cleaning	1.2	1.3	1.2	1.3	1.5
3 Washing	1.2	1.5	1.5	1.6	1.7
4 Ironing	0.6	0.6	0.8	0.9	1.0
5 Market	1.3	1.7	1.4	1.6	1.7
6 All domestic chores (1–5)	6.8	8.1	8.0	8.9	9.8
7 Collection of wood	0.4	0.2	0.2	0.2	0.1
8 Collection of water	0.8	0.9	0.9	0.7	0.8
9 Aid to other households	0.2	0.3	0.3	0.2	0.4
10 Community activities	0.2	0.3	0.3	0.2	0.4
11 Work for a wage	17.2	19.1	20.3	21.5	25.5
12 Work in a farm or family business	6.2	5.6	4.7	4.2	2.8
13 Work in labor market (11 + 12)	23.4	24.7	25.1	25.7	28.3
14 Total working time (definition 1)	31.4	33.9	34.1	35.4	39.0
15 Total working time (definition 2)	31.9	34.4	34.7	35.9	39.7
	Rural				
1 Cooking	5.2	5.2	5.7	5.5	5.7
2 Cleaning	1.5	1.8	1.9	1.8	1.8
3 Washing	2.0	2.0	2.2	2.2	2.1
4 Ironing	0.3	0.3	0.4	0.5	0.6
5 Market	1.9	1.9	2.2	1.9	2.2
6 All domestic chores (1–5)	10.9	11.3	12.4	11.9	12.4
7 Collection of wood	2.0	2.1	2.2	2.1	2.1
8 Collection of water	1.9	2.3	2.2	2.2	2.3
9 Aid to other households	1.0	1.0	1.1	1.1	1.1
10 Community activities	0.8	0.7	0.8	0.9	1.2
11 Work for a wage	7.2	9.3	10.6	11.7	15.9
12 Work in a farm of family business	25.9	23.8	22.1	20.5	16.4
13 Work in labor market (11 + 12)	33.1	33.1	32.7	32.2	32.3
14 Total time (definition 1)	47.9	48.7	49.4	48.3	49.2
15 Total time (definition 2)	49.7	50.5	51.3	50.3	51.5

Note: Zeros are included. Total time (definition 1) is the sum of 6 (all domestic chores), 7 (collection of wood), 8 (collection of water), and 13 (work in labor market). Total time (definition 2) is the sum of total time (definition 1), 9 (aid to other households), and 10 (community activities).

Source: Authors' estimates using EIBEP 2002–03.

same amount of time. The increase in the total consumption of household j that would follow is therefore:

$$\Delta C_j = \sum_{i=1}^{M}[[(T_{max} - T_i) \cdot m_i] \cdot \omega_i] \tag{1}$$

where T_{max} is the time poverty line or, in this context, a threshold of full employment in terms of the total number of hours worked (whether paid or unpaid), T_i is the time currently worked by individual i, m_i is an indicator equal to 1 if the individual is working a number of hours below the time poverty line, ω_i is the value of the time of individual i, and M is the total number of individuals in household j that can increase the total time worked. In order to run the simulations, we need to define T_{max}. Two standards were used for this purpose. The first one is a full employment work level defined arbitrarily at 50 hours a week; and the second one is a relative workload threshold set at 1.5 times the median of the total individual hour distribution, which turns out to be 70.5 hours.

The increase in per capita consumption of each member of household j can be re-written:

$$\frac{\Delta C_j}{N} = \frac{M}{N} \cdot \frac{\sum_{i=1}^{M}[(T_{max} - T_i) \cdot m_i]}{M} \cdot \frac{\sum_{i=1}^{M}[[(T_{max} - T_i) \cdot m_i] \cdot \omega_i]}{\sum_{i=1}^{M}[(T_{max} - T_i) \cdot m_i]} = \frac{M}{N} \cdot \overline{H}_M \cdot \overline{\omega}_M \tag{2}$$

where N is the household size ($N \geq M$). The above formulation is helpful because it highlights three possible sources of increase in per capita consumption: the ratio of non-time poor individuals with respect to the total (first term on the righthand side), the average number of extra-hours that each of the non-time poor individuals can work (second term) and the average value that each of these extra-hours can obtain (third term). When the calculation is made at the quintile level (the subscript j indicates the quintile rather than the household), the above decomposition gives us the average of each term for each quintile and their product gives the exact average of the increase in per capita consumption for all households in that quintile.

An empirical question is what value to assign to ω_i, the value of time of individual i. Here we have adopted three measures. A first candidate is the "potential wage" that each individual could earn in the labor market based on their personal and household characteristics. After estimating wage regressions separately for men and women (including the usual explanatory variables) we have predicted a wage for everybody in the sample. The estimates for the wage regressions are presented in Appendix Table 6.A1.[21] However, because the size of the formal labor market is small in Guinea, one can argue that few are the individuals who can increase their employment and be paid a wage for those extra hours. For this reason, we have created two additional measures of the value of one hour of work. First, we have divided

21. At this stage, the wage regressions have been estimated using the sample of individuals working for a wage, without correcting for selection for being in or out of the labor market. While other studies indicate that not correcting for selection is not likely to bias the coefficient in any substantial way, we face the problem of predicting the wage for individuals who are not working because many regressors are missing for them (for example, industry, type of employer, type of contract, and so forth). We have assigned to these individuals the median predicted wage of the groups defined by age, sex, maximum education level and urban and rural area.

the total household consumption by the total working time of all its members. This ratio can be considered a sort of "household consumption productivity" because it represents the efficiency of the household in translating each hour of work by any of its member into consumption. While this measure considers all household activities as "productive" and therefore able to generate consumption, it is true that extra employment aimed at increasing consumption would be mostly directed at the labor market and/or in farm or family business. Therefore we have also computed an alternative measure of "household consumption productivity" by dividing the total household consumption by the total number of hours spent by household members in the labor market (for a wage, in the informal labor market, or as contributing family members). In any case, it is clear from equation (2) that the choice of the threshold T_{max} and of the estimation of ω_i are crucial for the results we obtain.

Results

Impact on Consumption

We first calculated the impact on consumption, based on (1). The results are presented in Table 6.2, using both the predicted wage rate and the household productivity (definitions A and B) as the value of one hour of extra time in employment, and a full employment work threshold of 50 hours/week. When the predicted wage rate is used for ω_i (columns (3) and (4) in Table 6.2) the increase in consumption would be higher in the top than in the bottom of the distribution in absolute level, but larger in the bottom (and in the middle) of the distribution in relative terms. In this case the increase in employment would be essentially pro-poor.[22]

However, when each hour of extra-employment is evaluated using the household productivity (columns (5)–(6) and (7)–(8)), the increase in consumption is substantially higher in the top than in the bottom of the distribution and the increase in employment would result in a strong increase in inequality. In fact when the household productivity is used as a measure of the value of time, the increase in consumption is large at the upper tail of the distribution, especially when in the calculation of the household productivity only the time spent in the labor market is taken into account (definition B). Notice that when this latter measure is adopted, the increase in consumption in absolute terms in the bottom of the distribution is the largest (and therefore so is the reduction in poverty).

The fact that for the upper quintiles, we have a substantial divergence in the estimated values for ω_i implies that the impact on inequality of full employment will differ depending on the method used to evaluate the value of time. On the other hand, for the poverty simulations, what matters is the range of estimates in the bottom quintiles. Then, the magnitudes of the estimates from the two methods of estimation are fairly similar (when using the definition A of household productivity), so that the results are likely to be robust.

Table 6.3 gives us some clues about the main sources of the increase in consumption and the differences across quintiles. The bottom quintiles have the lowest amount

---

22. The increase in average consumption would be larger in the third than in the second quintile, though. As it will be shown later the interpretation of the impact on inequality differs somewhat depending on whether one looks at changes in the Gini coefficient or the Theil index, given that the two measures are more sensitive to changes in different parts of the distribution.

Table 6.2. Average Increase in per Capita Consumption Following an Increase in Individual Working Time, by Quintiles of per Capita Consumption (Full employment = 50 hours/week)

		Increase in per capita consumption					
		Evaluated at the wage rate		Evaluated at the household cons. productivity (A)		Evaluated at the household cons. productivity (B)	
Quintile of Cons.	Weekly Average per Capita Cons.	Average	%	Average	%	Average	%
(1)	(2)	(3)	(4)	(5)	(6)	(7)	(8)
1	3355	1010	30.1	959	28.6	1767	52.7
2	5465	1532	28.0	1931	35.3	3489	63.8
3	7642	2617	34.3	3310	43.3	5611	73.4
4	10801	3111	28.8	5823	53.9	9482	87.8
5	23288	3995	17.2	17045	73.2	22113	95.0

Note: See text in the "Analytical Framework" section for the definition of househld consumption productivity (A) and (B).
Source: Authors' estimates using EIBEP 2002–03.

of resources. The proportion of people that can increase their working time within a household as a proportion of household size is lower in the bottom than in the top of the distribution (26 percent in the bottom quintile versus 35 percent in the top quintile). Also, the average number of extra-hours that each individual below the full employment working hour threshold can work is lower in the bottom than in the top of the distribution (23 hours versus 30 hours). Finally, the value of one hour of time is higher for richer as compared to poorer individuals—twice as much for the top quintile with respect to the bottom in the case of the wage rate and as much as ten times in the case of the household productivity.

Table 6.3. Results of Decomposition for Full Sample (Full employment = 50 hours/week)

Quintile of Consumption	M/N	$\bar{H}_M$	$\bar{\omega}_M$ (Wage)	$\bar{\omega}_M$ (Household Consumption Productivity A)	$\bar{\omega}_M$ (Household Consumption Productivity B)
1	0.258	22.8	172	163	300
2	0.276	25.5	217	274	494
3	0.297	27.9	316	399	677
4	0.331	28.7	328	614	999
5	0.353	29.6	383	1634	2120

Note: See text in the "Analytical Framework" section for the Definition of househld consumption productivity (A) and (B).
Source: Authors' estimates using EIBEP 2002–03.

Table 6.4. Contribution of Men and Women to Average Increase in per Capita Consumption, by Quintiles of per Capita Consumption (At wage rate; full employment = 50 hours/week)

| Quintile of Consumption | Weekly Average per Capita Consumption | Increase in per capita consumption | | | |
| | | Men | | Women | |
		Average	%	Average	%
1	3355	631	18.8	380	11.3
2	5465	949	17.4	584	10.7
3	7642	1654	21.6	963	12.6
4	10801	1863	17.2	1248	11.6
5	23288	2403	10.3	1592	6.8

Source: Authors' estimates using EIBEP 2002–03.

All these factors contribute to the lowest increase in consumption (in absolute terms) in the bottom of the distribution. Note again that the average value of one hour calculated using the predicted wage and the household productivity (definition A) is very similar in the three bottom quintiles, even if the two values have been derived in two different and unrelated ways. The average value of one hour calculated as the household productivity definition B is higher than definition A, given that in the former case only the hours spent in the labor market are included in the denominator.

Tables 6.4 and 6.5 present the same exercise separately for men and women (using their respective wage rates).[23] As we could expect, the increase in consumption due to an increase in working hours by women would be substantially lower (30 to 40 per cent lower) than what an increase in employment by men could produce. What is surprising, though, is the sources of this difference as revealed by Table 6.4. Contrary to our expectations, the average number of individuals who can increase their hours of employment is almost the same for men and women in all quintiles. This result may seem in contrast with the "time poverty" estimates presented in Bardasi and Wodon (2005) in this volume. However, in part because there are more women than men in the total population of Guinea, the percentage of women who are not time poor over the whole population is almost the same as men's. Also, the average number of extra-hours that non-time poor individuals can add to what they work already does not differ much between men and women (we may overestimate however the ability of women to increase their working hours due to the fact that time spent for providing care is not recorder in the survey). Therefore, the differences between the sexes in the impact of higher working hours is driven almost entirely by the difference in their average wages, ranging from 20 to 44 percent less for women depending on the quintile (and much larger in the bottom than in the top of the distribution).[24]

---

23. The evaluation of the increase in consumption at the household productivity is less interesting in this case because this would be the same for both sexes.

24. Notice that this differential is not adjusted for characteristics, i.e. the average wage reflects both gender "adjusted" differentials and compositional effects.

Table 6.5. Results of Decomposition for Men and Women
(Full employment = 50 hours/week)

Quintile of Consumption	Men			Women		
	M/N	$\bar{H}_M$	$\bar{\omega}_M$	M/N	$\bar{H}_M$	$\bar{\omega}_M$
1	0.129	22.1	222	0.129	23.6	125
2	0.140	25.2	270	0.137	25.9	165
3	0.156	28.3	374	0.141	27.5	249
4	0.173	29.7	362	0.158	27.5	288
5	0.182	30.9	427	0.171	28.1	331

Source: Authors' estimates using EIBEP 2002–03.

As a robustness test, we report below (Tables 6.6 to 6.9) the same tables calculated using a much higher full employment workload threshold of 70.5 hours/week or 1.5 times the median of the individual total time distribution. Although the magnitude of the results changes (larger gains in consumption due to higher level of working hours), the conclusions are qualitatively very similar when comparing quintiles or sexes. For example, the difference in the contribution of men and women to the increase in consumption remains substantial, and also in this case it is mostly driven by differences in average wages.

Impact on Poverty and Inequality

Finally, we have computed the impact of the increase in consumption on poverty and inequality. The results are presented in Table 6.10. In the columns, the average total annual

Table 6.6 Average Increase in per Capita Consumption Following an Increase
in Individual Working Time, by Quintiles of Current per Capita
Consumption (Full employment = 70.5 hours/week)

		Increase in per capita consumption					
Quintile of Cons.	Weekly Average Per Capita Cons.	Evaluated at the wage rate		Evaluated at the household cons. productivity (A)		Evaluated at the household cons. productivity (B)	
		Average	%	Average	%	Average	%
(1)	(2)	(3)	(4)	(5)	(6)	(7)	(8)
1	3355	2546	75.9	2197	65.5	3835	114.3
2	5465	3542	64.8	4102	75.1	7197	131.7
3	7642	5566	72.8	6565	85.9	11085	145.1
4	10801	6741	62.4	11059	102.4	18132	167.9
5	23288	8938	38.4	30593	131.4	41731	179.2

Note: See text in the "Analytical Framework" section for the Definition of househld consumption productivity (A) and (B).
Source: Authors' estimates using EIBEP 2002–03.

Table 6.7. Results of the Decomposition for Full Sample
(Full employment = 70.5 hours/week)

Quintile of Consumption	M/N	$\bar{H}_M$	$\bar{\omega}_M$ (Wage)	$\bar{\omega}_M$ (Household consumption productivity A)	$\bar{\omega}_M$ (Household consumption productivity B)
1	0.409	31.5	198	171	298
2	0.429	33.6	246	284	499
3	0.450	35.7	347	409	691
4	0.485	37.1	374	614	1007
5	0.509	38.0	463	1583	2159

Note: See text in the "Analytical Framework" section for the Definition of househld consumption productivity (A) and (B).
Source: Authors' estimates using EIBEP 2002–03.

consumption has been computed for each quintile after the simulated increase, under the different assumptions about time poverty lines and values of ω_i. In the bottom of the Table, the "new" consumption poverty rate (headcount), Gini coefficient and Theil index are shown.

Clearly, the largest increase in consumption and decrease in poverty would be obtained when using a higher threshold for the level of working hours. However, even with the lower workload for full employment at 50 hours a week, the increase in consumption and reduction in poverty would be substantial (reduction in the share of the population in poverty by 10 to 15 percentage points). This shows that, even in the bottom of the distribution there are "unused" time resources that can be used to increase employment and the well-being of the household. At the same time, it is clear that poverty would remain massive in Guinea even if all individuals were working at the full employment level of 50 hours,

Table 6.8. Contribution of Men and Women to the Average Increase in per Capita Consumption, by Quintiles of Current per Capita Consumption
(At wage rate; full employment = 70.5 hours/week)

Quintile of Consumption	Weekly Average per Capita Consumption	Increase in per capita consumption			
		Men		Women	
		Average	%	Average	%
1	3355	1517	45.2	1029	30.7
2	5465	2108	38.6	1434	26.2
3	7642	3410	44.6	2156	28.2
4	10801	4083	37.8	2658	24.6
5	23288	5497	23.6	3442	14.8

Source: Authors' estimates using EIBEP 2002–03.

Table 6.9. **Results of Decomposition for Men and Women (Full employment = 75.0 hours/week)**

Quintile of Consumption	Men			Women		
	M/N	$\bar{H}_M$	$\bar{\omega}_M$	M/N	$\bar{H}_M$	$\bar{\omega}_M$
1	0.189	32.8	245	0.220	30.4	154
2	0.201	35.5	296	0.228	32.0	197
3	0.225	37.4	407	0.225	34.0	282
4	0.248	38.4	428	0.237	35.7	314
5	0.262	38.9	538	0.247	36.9	378

Source: Authors' estimates using EIBEP 2002–03.

or even 70.5 hours, so that an increase in labor at current wages and productivity level does not represent a magic bullet for the fight against poverty.

Note also that the monetary value of the extra hours is typically lower in the bottom than in the top of the consumption distribution, so that inequality tends to increase when approaching full employment. The exception is represented by the simulation that uses the predicted wage to evaluate one extra hour of employment (but even in this case, the Gini coefficient and the Theil index give opposite conclusions because consumption is increasing more in the third than in the second quintile in relative terms). When using the "household productivity" measure to value the additional hours of work assumed in the simulations, inequality is increasing substantially.

Table 6.10. **Increase in Average Consumption and Changes in Poverty Rate and Inequality Following an Increase in Individual Working Time Under Various Hypotheses**

Consumption Quintiles	Average per Capita Current Consumption	Full employment at 50 hrs/week			Full employment at 70.5 hrs/week		
		(At wage rate)	(At HH prod. A)	(At HH prod. B)	(At wage rate)	(At HH prod. A)	(At HH prod. B)
1	171316	223858	221181	262218	303695	285543	370737
2	284150	363839	384581	465580	468332	497455	658378
3	394745	530851	566864	686537	684162	736114	971154
4	559642	721402	862438	1052722	910172	1134718	1502527
5	1272735	1480456	2159070	2422609	1737529	2863585	3442761
Poverty rate	48.9	39.4	37.1	34.1	29.2	26.4	21.5
Gini coefficient	0.405	0.418	0.510	0.536	0.412	0.527	0.552
Theil index	0.331	0.321	0.612	0.592	0.299	0.657	0.631

Source: Authors' estimates using EIBEP 2002–03.

Conclusions

Conceptually, there could be two ways to rely on the labor of the poor to reduce poverty. One possibility would be to increase the productivity of that labor, so that the poor obtain higher wages or earnings from the effort they already put in. The second possibility is to increase the working hours of the poor, taking note of the fact that underemployment is pervasive in many countries. While it is true that many men and especially women already work long hours in Sub-Saharan Africa, in large part due to domestic chores and other household tasks, underemployment is nevertheless affecting a large share of the population. In addition, in most countries, because standards of living are so low and a large share of the population is poor, many individuals would like to work more in order to be able to improve their condition, even at low wage levels.

In this paper, we have not discussed what could actually be done in Guinea to improve employment prospects, both in terms of the availability of jobs and work, and in terms of the quality of those jobs. We have also not simulated how poverty could be reduced thanks to an increase in productivity that would lead to higher earnings or wages per hour of work for the population. Our aim has been rather modest, namely to estimate the reduction in consumption poverty that could be achieved if the adult population were working full time. Different thresholds were considered for what a full employment workload would be, and the magnitude of the reduction in poverty clearly depends on such thresholds. One key message is that job creation and full employment would lead to a significant reduction in poverty, even at the relatively low current levels of wages and earnings enjoyed by the population. Yet at the same time, poverty would remain massive even if all working age individuals would work full time.

In future work, the results obtained here could be compared to other results, such as the impact of an increase in productivity that would lead to higher hourly wages and earnings, or a shift in working hours within households to relieve the high burden placed on some members. What we hope to have demonstrated is that a time use approach to the analysis of employment is an attractive way to make the link between time use and consumption poverty, and that this type of simulation and results can be useful in thinking about the employment aspects of the poverty reduction strategies that many countries are now preparing, implementing, or revising.

References

Bardasi, E., and Q. Wodon. 2005. "Measuring Time Poverty and Analyzing its Determinants: Concepts and Application to Guinea." (Chapter 4 in this volume.)

Blackden, C.M., and C. Bhanu. 1999. *Gender, Growth, and Poverty Reduction*. Special Program of Assistance for Africa 1998 Status Report on Poverty, World Bank Technical Paper No. 428, Washington, D.C.

Buvinic, M., and G. Rao Gupta. 1997. "Female-Headed Households and Female-Maintained Families: Are They Worth Targeting to Reduce Poverty in Developing Countries." *Economic Development and Cultural Change* 45:2, 259–280.

Calvès, A.-E., and B. Schoumaker. 2004. "Deteriorating economic context and changing patterns of youth employment in urban Burkina Faso: 1980–2000." *World Development* 32:1341–1354.

Charmes, J. 2005. "A Review of Empirical Evidence on Time Use in Africa from UN-sponsored Surveys." (Chapter 3 of this volume.)

Dercon, S., and P. Krishnan. 2000. "Vulnerability, Seasonality and Poverty in Ethiopia." *Journal of Development Studies* 36:25–53.

Ellis, F. 2000. "The Determinants of Rural Livelihood Diversification in Developing Countries." *Journal of Agricultural Economics* 51:289–302.

Kanwar, S. 2004. "Seasonality and Wage Responsiveness in a Developing Agrarian Economy." *Oxford Bulletin of Economics and Statistics* 66:189–204.

Skoufias, E. 1993. "Seasonal Labor Utilization in Agriculture: Theory and Evidence from Agrarian Households in India." *American Journal of Agricultural Economics* 75:20–32.

Wodon, Q., and K. Beegle. 2005. "Labor Shortages Despite Underemployment? Seasonality in Time Use in Malawi." (Chapter 5 in this volume.)

World Bank. 2001. *Engendering Development: Through Gender Equality in Rights, Resources, and Voice.* World Bank Policy Research Report, Washington, D.C.

Appendix Table 6.A1. Wage Regressions, by Gender (Individuals aged 10+, not in school, who earn a wage or profit)

	Men	Women
Age	0.039***	0.037***
	(3.976)	(4.297)
Age squared	−0.000***	−0.000***
	(3.650)	(4.147)
Disabled (Base not disabled)	0.045	−0.180
	(0.334)	(0.994)
Marital Status (Base single)		
Monogamous	0.157**	0.183**
	(2.205)	(2.256)
Poligamous	0.373***	0.135
	(4.379)	(1.597)
Divorced	−0.111	0.216*
	(0.616)	(1.878)
Widow/widower	0.252	0.057
	(0.903)	(0.514)
Education Completed (Base none)		
Primary	0.211***	0.189**
	(3.131)	(2.232)
Secondary 1st	0.333***	0.288**
	(3.967)	(2.351)
Secondary 2nd	0.354**	0.268
	(2.016)	(0.666)
Technical	0.615***	0.656***
	(5.998)	(4.275)
University	0.742***	0.994***
	(7.759)	(4.432)
Industrial Sector (Base manufacturing)		
Agriculture	−0.801***	−1.112***
	(9.116)	(10.617)
Mines	0.727***	−0.039
	(5.299)	(0.185)
Energy	0.266	−1.742
	(0.838)	(1.326)
Construction	0.174	−0.415
	(1.624)	(0.703)
Trade	0.301***	−0.014
	(4.082)	(0.167)
Transport	0.266***	−0.011
	(2.746)	(0.032)
Finance, IT	−0.089	−0.286
	(0.544)	(0.929)

(*continued*)

Appendix Table 6.A1. Wage Regressions, By Gender (Individuals aged 10+, not in school, who earn a wage or profit) (*Continued*)

	Men	Women
Public admin, educ., health	−0.067	−0.399***
	(0.745)	(3.106)
Status in Employment (Base employee priv. sect., formal)		
Public employee	0.338***	0.219
	(3.395)	(1.172)
Employee priv. sect., inform.	−0.361***	−0.423**
	(3.212)	(2.127)
Self-employed	0.218**	−0.082
	(2.259)	(0.441)
Type of Contract (Base permanent)		
Seasonal	−0.309***	−0.165***
	(4.435)	(2.646)
Daily and piece work	−0.048	−0.066
	(0.722)	(1.035)
Rural (*base urban*)	−0.344***	−0.198***
	(5.326)	(3.032)
Geographical Area (Base Conakry)		
Boke	−0.005	−0.025
	(0.071)	(0.340)
Faranah	0.124	0.139*
	(1.575)	(1.832)
Kankan	0.015	0.068
	(0.174)	(0.799)
Kindia	0.041	−0.282***
	(0.503)	(3.513)
Labe	0.153*	0.105
	(1.704)	(1.088)
Mamou	0.376***	0.311***
	(3.835)	(3.303)
Nzerekore	−0.010	0.012
	(0.137)	(0.162)
Constant	5.210***	5.541***
	(23.790)	(22.038)
Observations	4350	4356
R-squared	0.276	0.239

Note: The dependent variable is the logarithm of the hourly wage, spatially adjusted (using poverty lines) for differences in purchasing power across regions; * significant at the 10% level, ** significant at the 5% level, ***significant at the 1% level.

Source: Authors' estimates using EIBEP 2002–03.

CHAPTER 7

Assessing the Welfare of Orphans in Rwanda: Poverty, Work, Schooling, and Health

Corinne Siaens, K. Subbarao and Quentin Wodon[25]

One of the aspects of the orphan crisis in Sub-Saharan Africa relates to time use, namely where orphans end up living and what they spend their time doing in their new household of adoption. While some orphans are welcomed in centres and institutions, many live with relatives or other members of their communities, and others are welcomed by families which are not directly related to them. Orphans are in many ways better off when welcomed by relatives or other families than when living by themselves or in institutions, but there are also concerns that the orphans (and especially girls) that are welcomed in some families may be required to provide more help for the domestic tasks to be performed, with the resulting time pressure in terms of workload preventing them from benefitting from the same opportunities in education and other aspects of their development as other children. The objective of this paper is to conduct preliminary work to test this assumption using recent household survey data from Rwanda, with an attention not only to traditional variables of interest such as school enrollment, child labor and time use, but also with an eye to assessing other dimensions of the children's welfare.

While there have been orphans in much of Africa for a long time in part due to a comparatively high incidence of conflicts, AIDS has swelled their number in many countries. According to a communiqué by UNICEF and UNAIDS (2003), the share orphans in Africa specifically due to HIV/AIDS has increased from 3.5 percent in 1990 to 32 percent in 2001. By 2010, the two agencies estimate that some 20 million

25. The authors are with the World Bank. This work was prepared as a contribution to the Poverty Assessment for Rwanda prepared at the World Bank. The authors acknowledge support from the Belgian Poverty Reduction Partnership for preparing this paper. Results from the paper were presented at a workshop organized in Kigali in March 2005 in collaboration with the government unit in charge of the country's Poverty Reduction Strategy. The views expressed here are those of the authors and need not reflect those of the World Bank, its Executive Directors or the countries they represent.

African children will have lost one or both parents to AIDS. According to UNICEF's Executive Director Carol Bellamy, "the crisis of orphans and other children made vulnerable by HIV/AIDS is massive, growing and long-term. But two-thirds of countries hard-hit by the disease do not have strategies to ensure the children affected grow up with even the bare minimum of protection and care."

Because of the legacy of the Genocide, the situation of orphans is perhaps more dramatic in Rwanda than in other countries. Even as the country has emerged out of conflict, the AIDS pandemic has begun to take a heavy toll of human lives, contributing significantly to adult mortality. How serious is the problem of orphans in Rwanda? Is it threatening the traditionally strong care-giving capacity of households and communities? Are orphans placed in fostering households well-protected, for example in terms of what is required to them for domestic work? Will the crisis of orphans in Rwanda threaten the attainment of human development goals especially the goals set for education, nutrition and poverty reduction? Finally, what is the role of public action to mitigate the crisis of orphans? While qualitative work has been done on the situation of orphans in Rwanda (Dona 2003), good quantitative evidence is still lacking to assess the situation. This paper aims to start to fill the gaps by providing partial answers to the above questions. These questions, in turn, are important for the broader purpose of this volume devoted to gender, time use, and poverty, because of the differences in the treatment of orphan girls and boys especially as it relates to time use, for example in the area of domestic work.

There are several reasons why orphans constitute an important development issue in Africa, and especially in Rwanda. We outline four such reasons here. First, the sheer numbers and the size of the problem threatens the traditional care-giving capacity of communities and households, in part because of the pressure that care-giving puts on the time available for other productive activities. This is already evident from both quantitative studies based on longitudinal data sets for Uganda (Deininger, Garcia, and Subbarao, 2003), and from a number of qualitative studies or situation analyses for various countries documented in Subbarao and Coury (2003).

Second, true to the African tradition, most orphans are placed either in extended families or in fostering households. Yet this communal arrangement, laudable as it is, may come at the cost of consumption shock to households who have taken in orphans. If the households that have absorbed orphans are already poor to begin with—and there is evidence to suggest that on average orphans in Africa live in poorer households compared with non-orphans (Case, Paxson, and Ableidinger 2002)—the consumption shock may translate into deeper poverty. Even if orphans are housed in relatively non-poor households as is the case in Rwanda, the consumption shock and consequential welfare loss may persist.

Third, faced with limited resources, one may expect fostering households to favor their biological children over fostered ones, denying orphans proper access to basic needs such as education, health care and nutrition. In Kampala, Uganda, 47 percent of households assisting orphans lacked money for education compared with 10 percent of apparently similar households not charged with the responsibility of caring for orphans (Muller and Abbas 1990). One out of seven children face this risk in Rwanda, with the potential of an erosion of the country's human capital, thereby jeopardizing the realization of millennium development goals.

Fourth, orphaned children face other related risks including child labor. Children living with sick parents, even before they are orphaned, may be pulled out of school to engage in household chores or economic activities. This risk may be particularly the case for orphaned girls. Evidence also suggests that the lack of parental protection and supervision may leave an open door for abuse, neglect and exploitation, and even violation of rights such as property grabbing (Subbarao and Coury 2003). Moreover, following parental deaths, some children may become household heads often with little skills to conduct the activities of a household head.

The implication of the above is that parental loss can have negative consequences for a household, the orphans, and the community at large. Figure 7.1 provides a simple diagrammatic representation of the key short- and longer-term impacts of parental loss on orphans themselves, the community, the host household as well as the broader economy. The costs to children include the strong possibility of dropping out of school, a decline in nutritional status, possible increase in child labor, potential loss of assets including land,

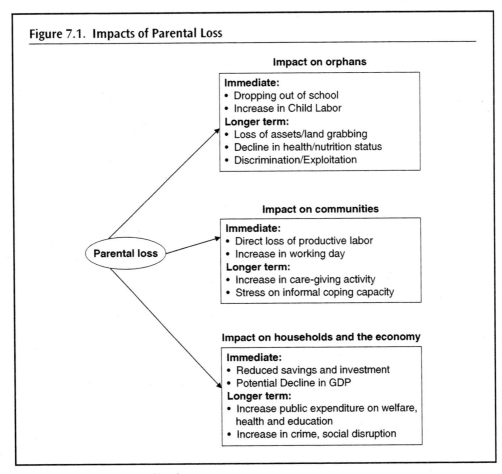

Figure 7.1. Impacts of Parental Loss

Impact on orphans

Immediate:
- Dropping out of school
- Increase in Child Labor

Longer term:
- Loss of assets/land grabbing
- Decline in health/nutrition status
- Discrimination/Exploitation

Impact on communities

Immediate:
- Direct loss of productive labor
- Increase in working day

Longer term:
- Increase in care-giving activity
- Stress on informal coping capacity

Parental loss

Impact on households and the economy

Immediate:
- Reduced savings and investment
- Potential Decline in GDP

Longer term:
- Increase public expenditure on welfare, health and education
- Increase in crime, social disruption

Source: Subbarao and Coury (2003).

and discrimination and exploitation. The costs to households and communities include the extra burden associated with the care-giving activity, a potential decline in available productive labor, and a general weakening of informal coping capacity. Few studies have set out to describe and quantify these impacts, especially the ones that arise in the short term (for example, the adverse schooling outcomes).

Full quantification of the different outcomes and channels through which the presence of orphans may affect welfare would require panel data that are not available for Rwanda. However, with the available data, namely a recent nationally-representative living standard measurement-type household survey, we are able to quantify the impacts of welcoming orphans on household consumption of fostering families, and the impact of being an orphan on schooling outcomes and work burden. The medium and longer term impacts on growth of orphans in Rwanda are beyond the scope of this paper.

The paper is structured as follows. The first section presents a broad quantitative picture of orphans in Rwanda, including a profile of orphans by age, gender and other characteristics. The second section assesses the impact of fostering orphans on the household consumption (and thereby on poverty) of foster families, and the impact on the child's education and nutrition outcomes of being an orphan. Conclusions and policy options are briefly discussed in the last section.

Number of Orphans and Qualitative Findings

Number of Orphans

As mentioned earlier, there are two main reasons explaining the high incidence of orphans in Rwanda. First, at least 800,000 people (10 percent of the population) died in the Genocide of 1994. While many of those who were left orphaned by the war have now reached adulthood, some are still under 15 years of age today, and since we use survey data for 1999–2001 for our analysis, the number of orphans from these events probably[26] remains large in our data. Second, AIDS in Rwanda as in much of Africa is also contributing to a high incidence of orphans.

Our empirical work is based on an analysis of the unit level data of Rwanda's *Enquête Intégrale sur les Conditions de Vie des ménages*. This is an Integrated Household Living Conditions Survey conducted between October 1999 and July 2001. Data collection in urban areas was carried out between October 1999 and December 2000. In rural areas, where 90 percent of the population lives, the survey was implemented from July 2000 to July 2001. When reporting results, we will consider the survey as representative of conditions as they stood in 2000–2001.

We will consider as orphans children who do not live with their mother, nor with their father. While this group may include some children who are not orphans, qualitative knowledge from the situation on the ground and a few simple data tests make us confident that this is a relatively good proxy. For example, although still very low overall, the share

---

26. Although we have a good handle on how to identify orphans in our survey data, we do not know why they are orphans, hence the use of "probably" in the above sentence.

Table 7.1. **Incidence of Orphanhood by Age, Area, and Poverty Status,**
          Rwanda 2000–01

	All	Urban	Rural	Poor	Non poor
	Age 0 to 6				
Double orphan	7.2%	7.3%	7.1%	7.2%	7.1%
Father is not in household	19.3%	21.9%	19.0%	23.2%	16.7%
Mother is not in household	1.6%	2.5%	1.5%	1.5%	1.8%
Both parents are in the household	71.9%	68.3%	72.3%	68.2%	74.5%
All children	100.0%	100.0%	100.0%	100.0%	100.0%
	Age 7 to 15				
Double orphan	18.4%	32.6%	16.9%	13.4%	23.1%
Father is not in household	28.4%	25.7%	28.6%	31.9%	25.1%
Mother is not in household	4.8%	4.7%	4.8%	4.1%	5.4%
Both parents are in the household	48.5%	37.0%	49.7%	50.6%	46.5%
All children	100.0%	100.0%	100.0%	100.0%	100.0%

Note: A child is defined as a double orphan when neither his father or his mother live in the same household.

Source: Authors' estimation using EICV 2000/01.

of so-defined orphans who benefit from a grant from Rwanda's Genocide Fund, a fund set up in the late 1990s to help the victims of the Genocide, is much higher among that group than among children who live with their mother, their father, or both. In any case, our definition implies that we are focusing our analysis on "double" orphans, that is, those that are likely to have lost both parents.[27]

In Table 7.1, the proportion of double orphans, as well as of orphans who are assumed to have lost only one parent (living with either their mother or their father, but not both) are shown in two age groups: 0–6 and 7–15. In these two age groups, respectively 7.2 percent and 18.4 percent are orphans. Thus, as in other countries, a large majority of orphans in our data fall in the age group 7–15. As mentioned earlier, this is due to both adult mortality due to AIDS and to the impact of the Genocide which was also felt at the time of the survey mostly in that age group.

A much higher percentage of children (19.3 percent and 28.4 percent respectively for the two age groups) have lost their father but not their mother, whereas the proportion of maternal orphans appears to be smaller (1.6 percent and 4.8 percent respectively). The reason

---

27. This does not mean that we minimize the adverse consequences on the child of loss of a single parent. A recent study for Zimbabwe had shown that children in the age group 13–15 who had lost their mothers were less likely to have completed primary school than children who lost their fathers, after controlling for other factors that influence primary school completion (Nyamukapa and Gregson 2003).

for a much higher percentage of paternal orphans is clearly the result of conflict which typically leads to higher adult male mortality in much of Africa, including in Rwanda. There are also rural-urban differences in the location of the 7 to 15 years orphans. In that age groups, a much higher percentage of orphans happen to be in urban areas than in rural areas, whereas there are no significant rural-urban differences in the proportion of children who have lost either parent under both age groups.

How do these estimates of the share of orphans compare with other estimates? According to UNAIDS, there could be up to 613,000 orphans due to AIDS only in the age group 0 to 14, or 17.5 percent of the child population. These estimates, which are very high, take into account both double and single orphans, and they would need to be increased further to take into account other orphans, mainly due to the Genocide. Using data from UNICEF's Multiple Indicator Cluster Survey for the year 2000, a recent World Bank report (2002) on education in Rwanda estimates that 28.5 percent of children were orphans, a proportion slightly below that of the UNAIDS estimate when Genocide orphans are taken into account.

Our own estimates in Table 7.1 are broadly similar to the estimates provided by UNAIDS and the World Bank education report, but because we will concentrate on double orphans in this paper, we will focus on a subset of the orphan population. Also, it is worth emphasizing that the AIDS prevalence may not have reached the high rates that were used until recently associated with Rwanda. Preliminary data from the 2004/05 Demographic and Health Survey suggests much lower rates of HIV prevalence than previously expected. This reduction in prevalence may reflect both an improvement in the quality of information and an indication that infection rates may actually have declined over time, especially in urban areas.

The bottom line is that the number of orphans in Rwanda is subject to debate, and the above estimates may actually be on the high side, essentially because the way to capture orphans in the survey used here relies on identifying children who do not live with any of their parents, but clearly some of these children may very well have one or both parents alive. The rest of the paper, which compares indicators of well-being between orphans and non-orphans and the key arguments made regarding these differences do not hinge on the actual number of orphans.

Qualitative Evidence on Living Conditions

A qualitative study of orphans was recently prepared for the Government of Rwanda, UNICEF and Save the Children Alliance (Dona 2003). According to this study, fostering a child can be a very spontaneous and informal decision but it can also take place through official placement networks. The likelihood of success is possibly higher in the case of organized fostering because it offers higher visibility and foster parents may have a longer-term vision for the child. Nevertheless, motivations and obligations are the same in both cases and, eventually, the impact for the parents will depend on their personal attitudes toward the child, on the child's integration with the siblings and on the child's own attitude.

Among the reasons why parents decide to foster, pity, social responsibility, loss of their own children, a desire to have children, and loneliness are frequently reported. After so much terror and pain in the country, people feel a common responsibility for each other.

"Children belong to us because all Rwandans have lost their own," said a parent. Apart from cultural, humanistic, and personal reasons, the need for assistance is also mentioned as a key reason for fostering. As a woman explained it, "As a widow, and only with boys, I needed a young girl that helped me in small domestic chores; you know, at a certain age, boys wander around [and] I was alone at home." While it is likely that the impact of fostering on the household will depend on the original motivations for fostering, the study suggests that "the fact that parents want to foster a child for help does not necessarily mean that the child was abused or exploited."

Fostering a child also has implications for household dynamics. The relationship with the siblings is most of the time perceived as good. Generally speaking, if there are adjustment difficulties, they are most prevalent at the beginning of the fostering process. Parents complain about the financial burden caused by fostering and about the lack of external assistance, but they seem to be generally happy and positive about the experience. They insist that the child is much better off with them than within a center. Still, foster parents are concerned about education and health, issues of identity, and the long-term future of the children they adopt, with some concerns about the financial resources needed to bring a child to maturity.

Overall, the study is rather positive regarding the ability of the fostering system to protect orphans. The study concludes that "the introduction of organized fostering programs has proved to be an appropriate means of providing family care for separated children unable to return to their own families," and adds that the "general impression [is] of fostered children being happy and well-integrated into their families." As we will see in the next section, the results of our own quantitative analysis are somewhat less optimistic, but this does not mean that they contradict the qualitative findings reported in Dona (2003). While orphans in foster homes may be at a disadvantage versus other children, they may still be much better off within foster homes than in orphanages. Interestingly, while spontaneous fostering was most prominent immediately after the Genocide, it gradually became less important than organized fostering. In the case of organized fostering, children who had been placed in a center are chosen by parents and must follow them and integrate a new family. Children in centers are waiting to be chosen, hoping to be well treated, to continue their studies, and to not be exploited. Dona's study thus concludes that in general children "find household chores a pleasant and rewarding activity." It helps them to be integrated in their new family. Of course, "Problems arise when children indicate that they work hard and when they say that they feel treated as unpaid servants." In other words, in some cases, foster children are clearly exploited or abused.

Living Conditions of Orphans: Quantitative Empirical Results

Household Consumption

An interesting aspect of the profile of orphans in Rwanda is that, no matter which age group one considers, a higher proportion lives in relatively non-poor households. This can be seen in Table 7.2. In fostering households as compared to households without orphans, consumption per equivalent adult, as well as the number of years of education of the head and spouse are all higher, while the unemployment rate for the household head is lower.

Table 7.2 Selected Characteristics of Households with and Without Orphans, Rwanda 2000–01

	Households with double orphans	Households without double orphans
Average yearly consumption per equivalent adult (Francs)	99,452	67,850
Population share in extreme poverty	32.0%	47.8%
Population share in poverty	45.8%	67.1%
Average size of land holdings (hectares)	0.8	0.7
Average number of infants (aged 0–4)	1.2	1.3
Average number of children (aged 4–14)	2.0	2.0
Average number of adults (aged 15 and above)	3.8	3.4
Share of households with female heads	28.2%	20.6%
Share of households without a spouse	32.4%	24.1%
Average number of years of education of household head	4.3	2.9
Average number of years of education of spouse	2.3	1.9
Share of household heads searching for employment	1.4%	2.8%
Population share living in urban areas	19.3%	8.4%

Note: A child is defined as a double orphan when neither his father or his mother live in the same household.
Source: Authors' estimation using EICV 2000/01.

Households with orphans are more often urban, female headed or more generally without a spouse for the household head. In fact, many double orphans are living in female-headed households where the female head is self-employed. This means that "self-selection" is going on, namely female-headed households working in informal sectors are probably the ones who are volunteering the most to take in orphans, presumably to get some help in domestic and economic work.

The fact that consumption is higher in households with orphans means that the probability of being poor is lower among those households. The poverty estimates used in Rwanda follow the measurement method adopted by the Government of Rwanda for the preparation of its Poverty Reduction Strategy. The method is explained in details in Ministry of Finance (2002). The share of the population in extreme poverty among households with orphans was 32.0 percent, versus a much higher 47.8 percent among households without orphans. Similarly, the respective shares of the population in poverty among the two groups are 45.8 percent and 67.1 percent. Addition all comparisons are given in the table in terms of landholdings and family size.

While households with orphans tend to be richer, welcoming an orphan is still likely to induce a loss in consumption for a household. According to preliminary estimates by Siaens and Wodon (2003), the marginal impact of having one orphan in the household on consumption is negative—estimated at the sample mean, there is a net reduction in per capita consumption of 5.2 percent and 11.5 percent in urban and rural areas respectively. Yet, some fostering households are fostering more than one orphan. When estimated for all orphans rather than for the addition of one orphan, the consumption shock is more severe: the net reductions in per capita adult equivalent consumption are 9.1 and 18.6 percent respectively for urban and rural areas. While these results should be considered as preliminary only,[28] they are in line with findings for Uganda, where Deininger, Garcia, and Subbarao (2003) also find a significant decrease in per capita consumption of fostering households in comparison with similar households not fostering orphans.

Thus, while fostering by households is an extremely important traditional safety net pervasive in Rwanda as in most other most African countries, its immediate consumption shock for the households who agree to foster cannot be ignored. Rwanda's Genocide Fund which provides grants to victims of the Genocide, including orphans, in order to help them with housing, education, and relocation expenditure may be a source of relief for fostering households, but unfortunately the data on such grants in the survey is weak, so that it cannot be used at this stage to assess the impact of the Fund on the fostering families and on the orphans' well-being.

Education and Child Labor

Being an orphan is associated with a lower probability of school enrollment. For the country as a whole, 76.4 percent of boys and 73.8 percent of girls in urban areas, and 67.7 percent and 67.2 percent in rural areas, are enrolled in school. The proportions for orphans are lower: 62.7 percent and 55.8 percent for boys and girls respectively in urban areas, and 61.5 percent and 62 percent in rural areas. Both male and female orphans have a lower probability of being enrolled in school, but the gap between orphans and non-orphans is larger for girls than for boys. Also, although present in rural areas, the gap in schooling for orphans is larger in urban areas, for both boys and girls. Table 7.3 also shows that a much higher proportion of both boys and girls are engaged in some form of non-domestic work, paid or unpaid, if they are orphans. In urban areas, the proportion of orphans engaged in work is twice as large for girls (31.6 percent) than for boys (18.4 percent). Orphans work also more at home in terms of hours per week than non-orphans. The difference between both groups of children is again higher in urban than in rural areas. Overall, it seems that some orphans, especially girls, are being fostered by female-headed households to share their work burden.

The fact that school enrollment is lower and the probability of working higher for orphans does not necessarily means that orphans are discriminated against in their foster

---

28. The results in Siaens and Wodon (2003) are based on regressions for the logarithm of consumption per equivalent adult on a wide range of household characteristics, including the presence of orphans. However, the number of orphans fostered by a household may itself depend on the level of well-being of the household before fostering, in which case we would have bias due to endogeneity. Nonetheless, controlling for other variables (education, age and gender of head, employment, location, and so forth), welcoming an orphan is still very likely indeed to reduce consumption per equivalent adult in a household because most of the impact on consumption comes through the increase in the number of equivalent adults due to fostering (that is, the number of infants and children increase).

Table 7.3. School Enrollment and Child Labor for Children Aged 7–15, Rwanda 2000–01

	All		Orphans		Non orphans		Head female				Head male	
							All kids		Orphans			
	Boys	Girls	Boys	Girls	Boys	Girls	Boys	Girls	Boys	Girls	Boys	Girls
Urban areas												
School enrollment rate	76.4%	73.8%	62.7%	55.8%	81.8%	84.1%	79.5%	74.5%	71.8%	58.8%	74.9%	73.5%
Working, paid or unpaid (except domestic work)	6.2%	12.3%	18.4%	31.6%	1.4%	1.3%	3.4%	11.5%	5.2%	25.3%	7.6%	12.7%
Domestic work (Hours/week)	6.38	14.80	10.03	22.76	4.94	10.27	5.90	15.14	6.85	20.56	6.61	14.62
Rural areas												
School enrollment rate	67.7%	67.2%	61.5%	62.0%	68.9%	68.2%	68.3%	67.9%	62.4%	64.3%	67.3%	66.7%
Working, paid or unpaid (except domestic work)	7.5%	7.2%	14.4%	10.6%	6.1%	6.5%	8.4%	7.5%	10.3%	10.4%	7.0%	7.1%
Domestic work (Hours/week)	6.84	10.34	7.48	11.46	6.71	10.11	6.71	10.36	7.14	11.17	6.91	10.32

Note: A child is defined as a double orphan when neither his father or his mother live in the same household.

Source: Authors' estimation using EICV 2000/01.

family. For example, orphans are on average older than other children, and this may explain part of the observed differentials in schooling and work. In order to assess whether orphans are less likely to be enrolled in school than other similar children who are not orphans, regression analysis is needed. Table 7.4 provides the results of probit regressions for the probability of enrollment in urban and rural separately, for boys and for girls. Controlling for a variety of child, household and community characteristics together with the education level and activity of the biological father and mother, the negative impact of being a double orphan is still strong.

Thus, with the important caveat that we cannot control for the orphan's life conditions just before fostering (for example, at the time of the parental loss, orphans may have dropped out of school and start working out of necessity, and it might be very difficult for these children to return to school even once they have found a foster family), the results in Table 7.4 are an indication that there is indeed some level of discrimination against the schooling of orphans in foster families.

Nutrition

Table 7.5 provides comparisons between orphans and non-orphans for selected health indicators, with a focus on children below five years of age. There are few differences in the probabilities of being sick, or to have had diarrhea over the last two weeks. However, orphans are less likely to have been vaccinated than any of the other groups identified in the table, and they are also less likely to benefit from a nutrition program. They are also less likely to have benefited from a postnatal consultation, or to have received vitamins A, than non-orphans children in the same households. Finally, the incidence of malnutrition (the probability of being stunted, wasted, or underweight) is also higher among orphans than among other children in the same households, but the measures are on par with the two other groups identified in the table.

The fact that many health indicators for young orphans are below those observed for other groups, especially other (biological) children living in foster families, again does not necessarily mean that there is a systematic discrimination against orphans in terms of healthcare and nutrition. It could be that orphans faced harsher situations before being welcomed in foster families. Malnutrition indicators often result from events early in life, which may have occurred before fostering. Still, the fact that orphans have lower rates of participation in nutrition programs than biological children in the same households, and that they have a lower probability of receiving vitamins A, begs questions as to whether they indeed receive equal treatment.

Conclusion

Because of the combined impact of the Genocide and the AIDS pandemic, the number of orphans (defined here as the children who live with neither their father nor their mother) is high in Rwanda. The results presented in this paper suggest that although orphans tend to live in foster households that are comparatively richer than the rest of the population, they are also less likely to go to school, more likely to work both at home and outside of the

Table 7.4. Determinants of School Enrollment among Children Aged 7–15, Rwanda 2000–01

	Urban areas				Rural areas			
	Boys		Girls		Boys		Girls	
	Coeff.	St. Er.	Coeff.	St. Er.	Coeff.	St. Er.	Coeff.	St. Er.
Characteristics of the Child								
Age	0.330*	0.056	0.341*	0.062	0.510*	0.032	0.535*	0.031
Age squared	−0.016*	0.003	−0.016*	0.003	−0.024*	0.001	−0.025*	0.001
Double orphan (no father and no mother)	−0.318*	0.096	−0.165*	0.079	−0.175*	0.063	−0.243*	0.061
No father only	−0.259*	0.107	−0.002	0.079	−0.015	0.061	−0.149*	0.060
No mother only	−0.208*	0.126	−0.159	0.152	−0.134*	0.053	−0.119*	0.056
Characteristics of the Household								
Migration (by the head, 5 years ago or more)	0.020	0.033	0.040	0.034	−0.003	0.018	0.014	0.017
Number of infants	0.041	0.047	−0.071	0.047	−0.048	0.026	−0.072*	0.024
Number of infants squared	−0.015	0.016	0.017	0.015	0.013	0.010	0.022*	0.009
Number of children	−0.048	0.042	0.044	0.036	−0.080*	0.027	−0.045	0.026
Number of children squared	0.013	0.007	−0.002	0.006	0.010*	0.005	0.006	0.005
Number of adults	0.026	0.024	−0.012	0.031	−0.023	0.020	−0.024	0.020
Number of adults squared	−0.002	0.002	0.002	0.003	0.004	0.003	0.007*	0.003
Household head female	0.153*	0.052	−0.004	0.079	0.138*	0.047	0.100*	0.048
No spouse in household	0.012	0.070	0.029	0.091	−0.103*	0.051	0.042	0.049
Education of Household Head								
Primary, not completed	0.088*	0.035	0.076	0.043	0.042*	0.019	0.059*	0.018
Primary completed	0.093*	0.035	0.067	0.047	0.086*	0.025	0.058*	0.025
Secondary, not completed	0.121*	0.038	0.110*	0.046	0.199*	0.032	0.104*	0.040
Secondary completed or superior	0.131*	0.035	0.092	0.054	0.196	0.075	0.154	0.079

Education of Spouse								
Primary, not completed	-0.032	0.063	-0.015	0.066	0.021	0.023	0.060*	0.022
Primary completed	-0.040	0.075	0.046	0.061	0.077*	0.034	0.100*	0.032
Secondary completed/superior	0.072	0.053	0.111	0.051	0.182*	0.043	0.103*	0.044
Employment of Household Head								
Does not work	0.067	0.041	-0.035	0.066	0.003	0.021	0.027	0.020
Works in industry/transport	0.044	0.049	-0.062	0.073	-0.075	0.070	0.047	0.062
Works in banking sector, or as professional	-0.013	0.061	-0.091	0.078	-0.033	0.077	0.098	0.057
Works in commerce	0.031	0.048	-0.135*	0.070	0.080	0.066	0.133	0.057
Works in other sectors, but not agriculture	-0.020	0.082	-0.156	0.106	-0.025	0.083	0.052	0.082
Education/Work of Biological Parents								
Biological father, primary not completed	0.045	0.058	0.054	0.057	0.087*	0.029	0.087*	0.028
Biological father, primary completed	0.100*	0.035	0.095	0.042	0.161*	0.026	0.118*	0.028
Biological father, secondary or superior	0.177*	0.029	0.117	0.049	0.175*	0.052	0.145*	0.052
Biological father, unstated education level	-0.031	0.080	-0.080	0.093	0.049	0.041	0.042	0.038
Biological mother, primary not completed	0.054	0.056	0.041	0.068	0.095*	0.040	0.077	0.040
Biological mother, primary completed or more	0.011	0.056	0.130*	0.040	0.154*	0.037	0.122*	0.039
Biological mother, unstated education level	0.059	0.069	0.051	0.075	0.039	0.053	-0.029	0.063
Biological father was in agriculture	-0.117*	0.059	-0.227*	0.056	-0.074	0.048	-0.016	0.044
Other Household Characteristics								
Number of hectares of exploited land	0.024	0.025	0.071*	0.032	0.017	0.012	0.035*	0.012
Number of hectares squared	-0.001	0.002	-0.007*	0.003	-0.001	0.001	-0.002	0.001
Head has health problems	-0.257*	0.159	0.153	0.052	0.007	0.039	-0.085*	0.041
Spouse has health problems	0.119	0.062	-0.001	0.157	0.057	0.066	-0.019	0.065

(continued)

Table 7.4. Determinants of School Enrollment Among Children Aged 7–15, Rwanda 2000–01 (Continued)

	Urban areas				Rural areas			
	Boys		Girls		Boys		Girls	
	Coeff.	St. Er.	Coeff.	St. Er.	Coeff.	St. Er.	Coeff.	St. Er.
Geographic Characteristics								
Kigali geographic dummy variable	-0.022	0.033	-0.048	0.033	0.015	0.029	0.062*	0.027
Population in locality (in millions)					0.000*	0.000	0.000*	0.000
Access to water in community					0.029	0.018	0.018	0.018
Access to electricity in community					0.046	0.031	0.051	0.028
Distance to market (in 100 km)					-0.002	0.002	0.000	0.002
Distance to road (in 100 km)					-0.016	0.009	-0.023*	0.009
Distance to primary school (in 100 km)					-0.018*	0.005	-0.017*	0.005
Distance to health center (in 100 km)					0.005*	0.002	-0.002	0.002

Note: A child is defined as a double orphan when neither his father or his mother live in the same household. Coefficients with * are significant at the 5 percent level. Coefficients underlined are significant at the 10 percent level. Omitted variables are: no education, agriculture, other regions than Kigali. Specification: probits.

Source: Authors' estimation using EICV 2000/01.

Table 7.5. Selected Health Indicators for Children Below 5 Years of Age, Rwanda 2000–01

	Single parent	Double orphan	Biparental child in fostering family	Biparental child in other families
			0–5 Years old	
Was sick in last 2 weeks	33.9%	30.1%	35.7%	33.3%
Received DTC vaccine	19.3%	13.9%	21.0%	16.9%
Received polio vaccine	24.0%	18.2%	25.4%	21.7%
Received rougeole vaccine	24.2%	19.8%	23.3%	24.4%
Received BCG vaccine	27.0%	15.1%	36.7%	31.0%
Received postnatal consultation	8.0%	8.8%	12.0%	8.1%
Had diarrhea in last 2 weeks	20.3%	19.1%	20.5%	20.5%
Receives A vitamins	9.4%	10.1%	13.2%	10.8%
Participates in nutrition program	19.9%	18.6%	28.8%	22.8%
			3–59 Months old	
Stunted (height for age)	38.4%	40.4%	26.0%	40.4%
Wasted (weight for height)	8.8%	6.8%	5.2%	6.6%
Underweighted (weight for age)	24.1%	23.5%	16.2%	26.6%

Note: A child is defined as a double orphan when neither his father or his mother live in the same household.
Source: Authors' estimation using EICV 2000/01.

home, less likely to be vaccinated, and more likely to suffer from health deficiencies. Thus, there is clear evidence that orphans are an especially vulnerable group of children in Rwanda.

The Government of Rwanda is aware of the plight of orphans, and policy interventions have been set up to help them. Funding for the Genocide Fund, which was created to benefit orphans from the Genocide as well as other victims from the conflict, is substantial, but it is unclear whether it reaches those who need help the most. The amounts in principle disbursed by the Fund are high, at about 10 percent of total recurrent spending for primary education, an amount also roughly similar to the total private spending on primary education in the country, including school fees. Yet, while some of this funding is supposed to provide schooling grants for orphan children, we do not find much evidence in the data that coverage is high.

The Government as well as NGOs are also aware that not all vulnerable children share the same history and face the same problems, and that this calls for differentiated policy responses. As noted in a recent Government report (MINALOC 2003), the war, the Genocide, poverty, and HIV/AIDS have created different forms of vulnerability. Some children lost their family and live in another household, or in special institutions or centers, or in the street. Others are disabled or affected by HIV/AIDS, and still others have problems with the justice, are mistreated, or are victims of sexual abuse. Some vulnerable children are working, live in an extremely poor household or are refugees. Each group faces specific problems and programs must be designed accordingly. General strategies to help meeting the needs of these various groups of children should also be implemented, but they are not enough by themselves. Such general strategies include actions for sensitization of the children, their parents and tutors, for example by promoting children's rights and informing on the existing policies and laws. Information campaigns can also help to show the impact of HIV/AIDS on the children. General strategies also involve building the necessary structures and human capacity to provide social protection and quality services to vulnerable children, with good coordination mechanisms between the different actors, in order to facilitate access for vulnerable children to basic services such as education, health, housing, income generating activities and credit (MINALOC 2003). In addition, inclusive sectoral level policy changes such as abolition of school fees may go a long way to promote enrollment of all children including orphans.

International experience can help in designing appropriate social protection mechanisms for orphans. Given the identified risk patterns, how can further changes in policy or programs ameliorate the observed vulnerabilities of orphans? Many questions regarding the appropriate type of assistance and the way it should be channeled remain open. Who should be targeted: the orphan, the fostering household, or communities? On what basis: the level of poverty, or risks of unmet basic needs including schooling? How should the transfer be channeled: cash or in-kind, and what would be an appropriate amount of transfer, and should transfer amount be uniform or adjusted to the needs? International experience especially in post-conflict countries such as Burundi and Eritrea suggest that publicly funded cash transfer program should be carefully designed to avoid stigma and adverse incentives (Subbarao and Coury 2003).

Based on this experience, and on Rwanda's own circumstances, at least four options seem to merit the attention of policymakers: (a) consider modifying the prevailing grant program into a conditional cash transfer program; (b) consider the scope for geographic targeting, using the school as the focal point for identification of eligible beneficiaries and transfer of assistance; (c) consider the scope for fostering grants to communities rather than directly to households; and (d) remove potential school-level barriers such as school fees and uniforms.

One way to improve the grant program would be to make it a conditional upon all children in the household, including fostered children, attending the school. There is now ample evidence from both low and middle income countries that transferring small amounts of cash to households conditional upon school attendance work, with small errors of exclusion and inclusion and cost-effective impacts. For a review of Mexico's PROGRESA, see for example Wodon and others (2003).

The risk of orphans dropping out of school or engaging in paid and unpaid work is more prevalent in urban areas than in rural areas, and in some provinces in rural areas. Given regional variations in the risks of orphanhood, another policy option could be to adopt a geographic targeting, or other forms of targeting. Resources could for example be transferred to schools located in the region/area in which orphans are at most risk of dropping out of school, with the responsibility to administer the grant program. Identification of eligible beneficiaries could then be done by a committee comprising of community leaders, school authorities, and the local government. This is along the lines of a program currently being administered in Zimbabwe. Information requirements for such a regional approach are reasonable.

Targeting "needy" orphans could be done based on (a) an enumeration of all needy children within a community, and (b) a devolution to the community of the selection of vulnerable children through some transparent process. Selection of needy children can be done through workshops and home visits by grassroots actors with the help of external support including prominent non-governmental agencies. In Burundi, for example, after a census of all needy children, communities came up with four categories of children: (a) double orphans who do not have any external support, (b) children separated from their parents and currently living in refugee camps or camps for displaced children, (c) single orphans that received no support from their surviving parent, and (d) double orphans living in very poor fostering households. Communities then began to prioritize and channel assistance to the above categories ranked by the degree of vulnerability. The main advantage of this type of channeling for assistance is that it avoids stigmatization; it does not, for instance, identify orphans by the nature of death of their parents (AIDS orphans are often stigmatized). Often the needy children need not necessarily be orphans; in South Africa "needy" children identified by communities turned out to be children of one important stigmatized group: teenage mothers. This method of channeling assistance may not work however where communities are divided along ethnic lines or if there is no community cohesion.

In a situation where the average access to education and other services is high, but there are differences in access between the poor and the non-poor, measures are needed at the sectoral/school level to improve access to services. Waiving school fees and uniform obligations has proven extremely helpful in Uganda; following this policy change, the discrimination against orphans in school enrollment has been completely wiped out in a period of five years. Similarly in the health sector, vaccination campaigns and nutrition supplementation programs would improve the general health of all orphans and vulnerable children.

Finally, beyond actions directly targeting orphans, it is also possible to think about the issues in a very different way, alongside the time use approach used in this volume. It has been argued that in at least some dimensions orphans may be better off when welcomed by relatives or other families than when living by themselves or in institutions. However, there are also concerns that the orphans (and especially girls) that are welcomed in some families may be required to provide a lot of help for the domestic tasks to be performed, with the resulting time pressure in terms of workload preventing them to benefit from the same opportunities in education and other aspects of their development as other children. If time is a key constraint in some of the households welcoming orphans, then policies aiming to reduce the time constraint may indirectly help orphans as well. The idea would be to investment in programs that would reduce the burden of domestic tasks, for example through the provision of infrastructure services (access to water and electricity) as well as labor-saving technology, among others for food processing. Policies reducing the transport time faced by households could also help to relax their time constraint.

All these suggestions should not be construed as recommendations for the Government of Rwanda. More detailed work would be needed before making such recommendations. The above suggestions are merely options among others, but the findings from this paper clearly suggest that something more should be done in order to better protect orphans in Rwanda, and part of this effort could deal with the time constraints faced by households welcoming orphans.

References

Case A., C. Paxson, and J. Ableidinger. 2002. "Orphans in Africa." Center for Health and Well-being, Research Program in Development Studies, Princeton University. Processed.

Dona, G., with C. Kalinganire and F. Muramutsa. 2003. "The Rwandan Experience of Fostering Separated Children." Kigali. Processed.

Muller O., and N. Abbas. 1990. "The Impact of AIDS Mortality on Children's Education in Kampala, Uganda." *AIDS Care* 2(1):77–80.

Deininger, K., M. Garcia, and K. Subbarao. 2003. "AIDS-Induced Orphanhood as a Systemic Shock: Magnitude, Impact and Program Interventions in Africa." *World Development* 31(7):1201–1220.

MINALOC (Ministère de l'Administration Locale, de l'Information et des Affaires Sociales). 2003. *Politique nationale pour les orphelins et autres enfants vulnérables*. Kigali.

Ministry of Finance. 2002. *A Profile of Poverty in Rwanda*. Kigali.

Nyamukapa, C., and S. Gregson. 2003. "Contrasting Primary School Outcomes of Paternal and Maternal Orphans in Manicaland, Zimbabwe: HIV/AIDS and Weaknesses in the Extended Family System." University of Zimbabwe. Processed.

Siaens, C., and Q. Wodon. 2003. "Determinants of Poverty in Rwanda." The World Bank, Washington, D.C. Processed.

Subbarao, K., and D. Coury. 2003. "Orphans in Sub Saharan Countries: A Framework for Public Action." The World Bank, Washington, D.C. Processed.

UNICEF and UNAIDS. 2003. "UNICEF and UNAIDS Applaud Milestone in Forging Coordinated Global Response to Growing Crisis of Children Orphaned Due to AIDS." Press Release of October 21. Geneva.

Wodon, Q., B. de la Briere, C. Siaens, and S. Yitzhaki. 2003. "The Impact of Public Transfers on Inequality and Social Welfare: Comparing Mexico's PROGRESA to Other Government Programs." *Research on Economic Inequality* 10:147–171.

World Bank. 2003. *Education in Rwanda: Accelerating the Agenda for Post-Conflict Development*. Washington, DC.

Eco-Audit

Environmental Benefits Statement

The World Bank is committed to preserving Endangered Forests and natural resources. We print World Bank Working Papers and Country Studies on 100 percent postconsumer recycled paper, processed chlorine free. The World Bank has formally agreed to follow the recommended standards for paper usage set by Green Press Initiative—a nonprofit program supporting publishers in using fiber that is not sourced from Endangered Forests. For more information, visit www.greenpressinitiative.org.

In 2004, the printing of these books on recycled paper saved the following:

Trees*	Solid Waste	Water	Net Greenhouse Gases	Electricity
307	14,387	130,496	28,262	52,480
'40' in height and 6-8" in diameter	Pounds	Gallons	Pounds	KWH